A Love Letter to Mary

Keith Berubé

En Route Books and Media, LLC
St. Louis, MO

En Route Books and Media, LLC

5705 Rhodes Avenue

St. Louis, MO 63109

Cover credit: TJ Burdick from Juan Carreño de Miranda. *Saint Anne Teaching the Virgin to Read*. Circa 1676.

Library of Congress Control Number: 2020947904

ISBN: 978-1-952464-32-4 and 978-1-952464-33-1

Dedication

ad mea puella: mea dulcis Virgo Maria

Quam pulchra es, amica mea! quam pulchra es! Oculi tui columbarum, absque eo quod intrinsecus latet. Sicut vitta coccinea labia tua, et eloquium tuum dulce. Sicut fragmen mali punici, ita genae tuae, absque eo quod intrinsecus latet. Tota pulchra es, amica mea, et macula non est in te. Vulnerasti cor meum, soror mea, sponsa; vulnerasti cor meum in uno oculorum tuorum, et in uno crine colli tui. Favus distillans labia tua, sponsa; mel et lac sub lingua tua: et odor vestimentorum tuorum sicut odor thuris. Hortus conclusus soror mea, sponsa, hortus conclusus, fons signatus.

How beautiful art thou, my love, how beautiful art thou! thy eyes are doves' eyes, besides what is hid within. Thy lips are as a scarlet lace: and thy speech sweet. Thy cheeks are as a piece of a pomegranate, besides that which lieth hid within. Thou art all fair, O my love, and there is not a spot in thee. Thou hast wounded my heart, my sister, my spouse, thou hast wounded my heart with one of thy eyes, and with one hair of thy neck. Thy lips, my spouse, are as a dropping honeycomb, honey and milk are under thy tongue; and the smell of thy garments, as the smell of frankincense. My sister, my spouse, is a garden enclosed, a garden enclosed, a fountain sealed up.

~Canticle of Canticles, chapter 4

Alexandre-François Caminade. *The Marriage of the Virgin*. 1824.

In honour of St. Philomena

Giuseppe Bezzuoli. *Santa Filomena*. 1840.

Table of Contents

About this Book

The Holy Trinity is absolutely enamoured of Mary. The Saints and so many good Catholics not canonized are totally in love with Mary. Both God and man have expressed their hearts for Mary in poetic ways. When these expressions of love are placed together, what appears is one vast love letter to Mary, one letter comprised of countless letters, like thousands of shards of a great mirror each reflecting with more or less intensity the loveliest, sweetest light. God desires this mirror. He wants to express in creation, in Scripture, and in the lives of all those who love her His infinite, eternal, unfathomable, and fiery love for Mary, each saint contributing to this love letter in his or her own absolutely unique, incommunicable way. Of course so much of this love letter resides in the abyss of the heart where there are, finally, no adequate words; the expressions of love that we do have for Mary, as written in this book, are like the froth of ocean waves, merely hinting at the tremendous depths that lay beneath.

Yet not all means of saying "I love you!" are composed of letters; sometimes, the medium is color. Thus throughout this little book there are scattered abundant paintings, most of them *directly* meant to be love letters to Mary in portraiture, though some are *indirect*—paintings not intended by the artist to represent Mary, but such that the images evoke Mary in some measure, expressing the innate desire of all hearts to love her. Keeping in mind Venerable Fulton Sheen's words—"She is the one whom every man loves when he loves a woman—whether he knows it or not. She is what every woman wants to be when she looks at herself"[1]—every painting that could be seen as an unintentional portrayal of Mary reveals the hidden recesses of

---

[1] Fulton Sheen, *The World's First Love* (San Francisco: Ignatius, 2010), 24.

the heart, hearts that long for her but may not know that Mary is the perfect woman for whom they long.

And while the words and paintings of others are not directly our own, they nevertheless express something of what is in our hearts, too, and we can *make them our own*. Thus, this little book is not merely a compilation of expressions of love for Mary, it forms one whole, a united love letter to Mary, filled with words that find a resonance in our own hearts. In other words, there is a sympathetic vibration in our hearts with all that the Holy Trinity, the saints, and others have expressed about Mary such that each person can take any number of these declarations of love for her, or all of them, and spin them into a new and unique letter from one's own heart, adding one's own unique inflection and sentiments to the words, one's own harmonies and melodies woven into a great symphony of love for Mary, in this way contributing to a great tapestry whereupon one gazes at Mary and says "I love you" in ever new ways. It's a romance (as a few of those in this book directly and unabashedly reveal)…each person participating in his or her own way in the Holy Trinity's own romance with Mary—and heart speaks to heart, *cor ad cor loquitur*.

Make this book your own, use it to express your own love for Mary and to increase your bond with her, say the words herein to Mary yourself, add to them by jotting down ideas in the margins and white spaces (I suggest using a pencil—you may at some point want to add or subtract, make more space, or erase sentiments you want no one else to know). There are blank pages in the back of the book as well for longer thoughts, letters, and ramblings of the heart.

> The mind is infinitely variable in its language, but the heart
> is not. The heart of a man, in the face of the woman he loves,
> is too poor to translate the infinity of affection into a differ-

ent word. So the heart takes one expression, 'I love you,' and in saying it over and over again, it never repeats.[2]

A Short Note about the Choices for this Text

The "love letters" to Mary crafted over the millennia could be multiplied many times over, filling practically infinite volumes. "Nineteen centuries," wrote Louis Kaczmarek, "have not been sufficient to recount the magnificence of Mary."[3] This present book is a mere sampling of some of the best words about Mary, a short but cohesive love letter unto itself. Never will one book, or a world full of books, be able to comprehend the love that men and angels have for Mary, let alone comprehend God's love for her. Ultimately, all love letters to Mary terminate in the most tender, affectionate and impassioned sighs of the heart, a joyful attempt to express an incomprehensible love.

A Final Note about the Format

In the first part of the first section, "Our Love Letter to Mary," I have omitted quotation marks so as to provide a more seamless presentation of biblical texts and to better integrate the words of Mary to saints and the quotes from the saints themselves; thus, the headings in bold relate who is speaking.

In the second part of the first section there are also headings in bold, but I have retained the use of quotation marks so as to avoid confusion as there are frequently several quotes from one person, quotes all related to Mary, but not all related directly one to another.

---

[2] Donald Calloway, *Champions of the Rosary: The History and Heroes of a Spiritual Weapon* (Stockbridge, MA: Marian, 2016), 311.

[3] Louis Kaczmarek, *Mary and the Power of God's Love* (Manassas, VA: Trinity, 1988), 126.

In section II, "Mary's Love Letter to Us," I have followed the same format as in section I: no quotation marks for the biblical passages, but employing quotation marks for non-biblical quotes as in the second part of the first section, while headings set off the quotes one from another.

For poems, I have not included quotation marks, only a heading.

Section 1

A Love Letter to Mary

I

God's Love Letter to Mary

Old Testament

Introduction

In the Old Testament, we find many descriptions of Mary, a sort of preparation for her arrival at the fullness of time. Many of these descriptions come from "types" of Mary, historical women in their own right with their own role in salvation history. These women reflect Mary, point to her, "prefiguring" her, supplying crucial descriptions of her: the beauty of body and soul of these Old Testament women is possessed by Mary in perfection and to the highest possible degree. One Old Testament type, however, is not a historical person and seems to be an almost direct revelation of Mary: Lady Wisdom. In fact, the historical women who are types of Mary build up toward and lead to this mysterious Lady Wisdom, who comes as a culmination of Old Testament hints of Mary, each of them being a sort of melody of God's love for her. By the time we get to the New Testament, not much detail of Mary is needed since so much has been revealed already in the Old Testament; finding her in the Gospels we say, "Hey, I know this Girl!"

Venerable Fulton Sheen, on Proverbs 8

In a particular way, He created His own Mother. He thought of her before she was born, as the poet thinks of his poem before it is written. He conceived her in His eternal mind before she was conceived in the womb of her mother, Saint Ann. In an improper sense, when she was conceived eternally in the pure mind of God, that was her first "Immaculate Conception." In the Mass of that feast, the Church puts into her mouth the words from the Book of Proverbs, saying that from all eternity God had thought of her, even before the mountains were raised and the valleys were leveled.

The Lord made me his when first he went about his work, at the birth of time, before his creation began. Long, long ago, before earth was fashioned, I held my course. Already I lay in the womb, when the depths were not yet in being, when no springs of water had yet broken; when I was born, the mountains had not yet sunk on their firm foundations, and there were no hills; not yet had he made the earth, or the rivers, or the solid framework of the world. I was there when he built the heavens, when he fenced in the waters with a vault inviolable, when he fixed the sky overhead, and leveled the fountain-springs of the deep. I was there when he enclosed the sea within its confines, forbidding the waters to transgress their assigned limits, when he poised the foundations of the world. I was at his side, a master workman, my delight increasing with each day, as I made play before him all the while; made play in this world of dust, with the sons of Adam for my play-fellows. Listen to me, then, you that are my sons, that follow, to your happiness, in the paths I show you; listen to the teaching that will make you wise, instead of turning away from it. Blessed are they who listen to me, keep vigil, day by day, at my threshold, watching till I open my doors. The man who wins me, wins life, drinks deep of the Lord's favor; who fails,

fails at his own bitter cost; to be my enemy is to be in love with death [Proverbs 8:22-36].

But God not only "thought" about Mary. He actually created her soul and infused it into a body, co-created by her parents. It was through her portals as the Gate of Heaven that He would come into the world. If God labored six days in preparing a paradise for man, He would spend a longer time preparing a paradise for His Divine Son. As no weeds grew in Eden, so no sin would arise in Mary, the paradise of the Incarnation.[4]

Toby Edward Rosenthal. *His Madonna*. 1908.

---

[4] Fulton Sheen, "Mary, Motherhood and the Home," Catholic Truth Society of Oregon No. Fam049 (1952), at http://pamphlets.org.au.

St. Nicholas of Flüe

Now I want to speak to you also about the pure servant-girl Mary who is yet a Queen of Heaven and earth and who was foreseen by Divine Wisdom. The same invested her as soon as God decided to create her. So she was conceived in the mind of the All-High Lord before she was conceived in her Mother's womb. And the same grace was in that union with great sanctity. That is why she is pure, gentle and immaculate.[5]

Edmund Blair Leighton. *The King and the Beggar-Maid.* 1898.

---

[5] Raphael Brown, *Saints Who Saw Mary* (Charlotte, NC: TAN, 2012), 98-99.

Rebecca

An exceeding comely maid, and a most beautiful virgin, and not known to man.[6]

Rachel

Rachel was well favoured, and of a beautiful countenance. And Jacob being in love with her, said: I will serve thee seven years for Rachel thy younger daughter.[7]

Judith

And she was exceedingly beautiful…And she was greatly renowned among all, because she feared the Lord very much, neither was there any one that spoke an ill word of her.[8]

And she washed her body, and anointed herself with the best ointment, and plaited the hair of her head, and put a bonnet upon her head, and clothed herself with the garments of her gladness, and put sandals on her feet, and took her bracelets, and lilies, and earlets, and rings, and adorned herself with all her ornaments. And the Lord also gave her more beauty: because all this dressing up did not proceed from sensuality, lent from virtue: and therefore the Lord increased this her beauty, so that she appeared to all men's eyes incomparably lovely….And when they saw her they were astonished, and admired her beauty exceedingly.[9]

And when the men [the Assyrian watchmen, enemies of God's people, to whom Judith went in order to slay the general of their army] had heard

---

[6] Genesis 24:16-20.
[7] Genesis 29:17, 18.
[8] Judith 8:7,8.
[9] Judith 10:3-8.

her words, they beheld her face, and their eyes were amazed, for they wondered exceedingly at her beauty.[10]

…and they admired her wisdom, and they said one to another: There is not such another woman upon earth in look, in beauty, and in sense of words.[11]

She anointed her face with ointment, and bound up her locks with a crown, she took a new robe to deceive him [Holofernes, Assyrian army general]. Her sandals ravished his eyes, her beauty made his soul her captive…[12]

…she went to the pillar that was at his bed's head [Holofernes], and loosed his sword that hung tied upon it. And when she had drawn it out, she took him by the hair of his head, and said: Strengthen me, O Lord God, at this hour. And she struck twice upon his neck, and cut off his head, and took off his canopy from the pillars, and rolled away his headless body.

And after a while she went out, and delivered the head of Holofernes to her maid, and bade her put it into her wallet. And they two went out according to their custom, as it were to prayer, and they passed the camp, and having compassed the valley, they came to the gate of the city. And Judith from afar off cried to the watchmen upon the walls: Open the gates for God is with us, who hath shewn his power in Israel. And it came to pass, when the men had heard her voice, that they called the ancients of the city. And all ran to meet her from the least to the greatest: for they now had no hopes that she would come.

And lighting up lights they all gathered round about her: and she went up to a higher place, and commanded silence to be made. And when all had held their peace, Judith said: Praise be the Lord our God, who hath not forsaken them that hope in him. And by me his handmaid he hath fulfilled

---

[10] Judith 10:14.
[11] Judith 11:19.
[12] Judith 16:10,11.

his mercy, which he promised to the house of Israel: and he hath killed the enemy of his people by my hand this night.[13]

…Blessed art thou, O daughter, by the Lord the most high God, above all women upon the earth. Blessed be the Lord who made heaven and earth, who hath directed thee to the cutting off the head of the prince of our enemies. Because he hath so magnified thy name this day, that thy praise shall not depart out of the mouth of men who shall be mindful of the power of the Lord forever, for that thou hast not spared thy life, by reason of the distress and tribulation of thy people, but hast prevented our ruin in the presence of our God.[14]

And Joachim the high priest came from Jerusalem to Bethulia with all his ancients to see Judith. And when she was come out to him, they all blessed her with one voice, saying: Thou art the glory of Jerusalem, thou art the joy of Israel, thou art the honour of our people: For thou hast done manfully, and thy heart has been strengthened, because thou hast loved chastity, and after thy husband hast not known any other: therefore also the hand of the Lord hath strengthened thee, and therefore thou shalt be blessed for ever. And all the people said: So be it, so be it.[15]

Esther

For she was exceeding fair, and her incredible beauty made her appear agreeable and amiable in the eyes of all.[16] [She had] a rosy colour in her face…gracious and bright eyes.[17]

---

[13] Judith 13:8-18.
[14] Judith 13:23-25.
[15] Judith15: 9-12.
[16] Esther 2:15.
[17] Esther 15:8.

Lady Wisdom

And I preferred her before kingdoms and thrones, and esteemed riches nothing in comparison of her. Neither did I compare unto her any precious stone: for all gold in comparison of her, is as a little sand, and silver in respect to her shall be counted as clay. I loved her above health and beauty, and chose to have her instead of light: for her light cannot be put out. Now all good things came to me together with her, and innumerable riches through her hands.[18]

For she is an infinite treasure to men! Which they that use, become the friends of God.[19]

For in her is the spirit of understanding: holy, one, manifold, subtile, eloquent, active, undefiled, sure, sweet, loving that which is good, quick, which nothing hindereth, beneficent, Gentle, kind, steadfast, assured, secure, having all power, overseeing all things, and containing all spirits, intelligible, pure, subtile. For wisdom is more active than all active things: and reacheth everywhere by reason of her purity. For she is a vapour of the power of God, and a certain pure emanation of the glory of the almighty God: and therefore no defiled thing cometh into her.

For she is the brightness of eternal light, and the unspotted mirror of God's majesty, and the image of his goodness. And being but one, she can do all things: and remaining in herself the same, she reneweth all things, and through nations conveyeth herself into holy souls, she maketh the friends of God and prophets. For God loveth none but him that dwelleth with wisdom. For she is more beautiful than the sun, and above all the order of the stars: being compared with the light, she is found before it. For after this cometh night, but no evil can overcome wisdom.[20]

---

[18] Wisdom 7:8-11.
[19] Wisdom 7:14.
[20] Wisdom 7:22-30.

Say to wisdom: Thou art my sister[21]

Say, therefore, I pray thee, that thou art my sister: that I may be well used for thee, and that my soul may live for thy sake.[22]

Thou art our sister, mayst thou increase to thousands of thousands, and may thy seed possess the gates of their enemies.[23]

Forsake her not, and she shall keep thee: love her, and she shall preserve thee.[24]

Take hold on her, and she shall exalt thee: thou shalt be glorified by her, when thou shalt embrace her.[25]

She reacheth therefore from end to end mightily, and ordereth all things sweetly.[26]

Her have I loved, and have sought her out from my youth, and have desired to take her for my spouse, and I became a lover of her beauty.[27]

I purposed therefore to take her to me to live with me: knowing that she will communicate to me of her good things, and will be a comfort in my cares and grief. For her sake I shall have glory among the multitude, and honour with the ancients, though I be young...[28]

When I go into my house, I shall repose myself with her: for her conversation hath no bitterness, nor her company any tediousness, but joy and gladness. Thinking these things with myself, and pondering them in my heart, that to be allied to wisdom is immortality, And that there is great delight in her friendship, and inexhaustible riches in the works of her hands, and in the exercise of conference with her, wisdom, and glory in the

---

[21] Proverbs 7:4.
[22] Genesis 12:13.
[23] Genesis 24:60.
[24] Proverbs 4:6.
[25] Proverbs 4:8.
[26] Wisdom 8:1.
[27] Wisdom 8:2.
[28] Widoms 8:9.

communication of her words: I went about seeking, that I might take her to myself.[29]

Send her out of thy holy heaven, and from the throne of thy majesty, that she may be with me and may labour with me, that I may know what is acceptable with thee…[30]

For she knoweth and understandeth all things, and shall lead me soberly in my works, and shall preserve me by her power. So shall my works be acceptable.[31]

He created her in the Holy Ghost, and saw her, and numbered her, and measured her. And he poured her out upon all his works, and upon all flesh according to his gift, and hath given her to them that love him.[32]

She will come to meet him like a mother, and like the wife of his youth she will welcome him.[33]

They that hold her fast, shall inherit life: and whithersoever she entereth, God will give a blessing. They that serve her, shall be servants to the holy one: and God loveth them that love her…he that looketh upon her, shall remain secure. If he trust to her, he shall inherit her.[34]

Come to her with all thy mind, and keep her ways with all thy power. Search for her, and she shall be made known to thee, and when thou hast gotten her, let her not go: For in the latter end thou shalt find rest in her, and she shall be turned to thy joy.[35]

My dove in the clefts of the rock, in the hollow places of the wall, shew me thy face, let thy voice sound in my ears: for thy voice is sweet, and thy face comely.[36]

---

[29] Wisdom 8:16-18.
[30] Wisdom 9:10.
[31] Wisdom 9:11-12.
[32] Ecclesiasticus 1:9-10.
[33] Sirach 15:2.
[34] Sirach 4:14-17.
[35] Sirach 6:27-29.
[36] Song of Songs 2:14.

Thou art all fair, O my love, and there is not a spot in thee…Thou hast wounded my heart, my sister, my spouse.[37]

How beautiful art thou, my love, how beautiful art thou! Thy eyes are doves' eyes, besides what is hid within… My sister, my spouse, is a garden enclosed, a garden enclosed, a fountain sealed up.[38]

Who is she that goeth up by the desert, as a pillar of smoke of aromatical spices, of myrrh, and frankincense, and of all the powders of the perfumer?…[39] and the sweet smell of thy ointments above all aromatical spices,[40] the smell of thy garments, as the smell of frankincense.[41] Cypress with spikenard. Spikenard and saffron, sweet cane and cinnamon, with all the trees of Libanus, myrrh and aloes with all the chief perfumes…[42]

…thy speech [is] sweet,[43] the odour of thy mouth like apples.[44]

…Thy lips are as a scarlet lace,[45] and Thy lips, my spouse, are as a dropping honeycomb, honey and milk are under thy tongue.[46]

Behold thou art fair, my beloved, and comely.[47] Thy cheeks are as a piece of a pomegranate, besides that which lieth hid within.[48] Thou art all fair, O my love, and there is not a spot in thee.[49] Thou hast wounded my heart, my sister, my spouse, thou hast wounded my heart with one of thy eyes, and with one hair of thy neck.[50] One is my dove, my perfect one is but one.[51]

---

[37] Song of Songs 4:7, 9.
[38] Song of Songs 4:1, 12.
[39] Song of Songs 3:6.
[40] Song of Songs 4:10.
[41] Song of Songs 4:11.
[42] Song of Songs 4:13-14.
[43] Song of Songs 4:3.
[44] Song of Songs 7:8.
[45] Song of Songs 4:3.
[46] Song of Songs 4:11.
[47] Song of Songs 1:15.
[48] Song of Songs 4:3.
[49] Song of Songs 4:7.
[50] Song of Songs 4:9.
[51] Song of Songs 6:8.

New Testament

Venerable Mary of Agreda, on Mary Prior to the Annunciation

…Mary heard God say to her: 'Our Chosen Dove, We wish to accept thee anew as Our Bride, and therefore We wish to adorn thee worthily.' As Mary abased herself with charming modesty, two seraphim proceeded to vest her with a beautiful white robe and bejeweled girdle, golden hair clasp, sandals, bracelets, rings, earrings and a necklace—all symbolizing the various virtues that adorned her lovely soul.[52]

Franz Xaver Winterhalter. *Leonilla, Princess of Sayn-Wittgentein-Sayn.* 1843.

---

[52] Raphael Brown, *The Life of Mary as Seen by the Mystics* (Charlotte, NC: TAN, 2012), 72.
[This book is a compilation that draws from the mystic visions of Mary's life as seen by St. Elizabeth of Schoenau, St. Bridget of Sweden, Venerable Mary of Agreda and Blessed Anne Catherine Emmerich.]

St. Bonaventure, on Mary Prior to the Annunciation

> O Mary, full thou art, of the unction of mercy,
> And of oil, compassionate. The King falls in love
> With your beauty—without—But greater—within.[53]

The Annunciation

And in the sixth month, the angel Gabriel was sent from God into a city of Galilee, called Nazareth, To a virgin espoused to a man whose name was Joseph, of the house of David; and the virgin's name was Mary. And the angel being come in, said unto her: Hail, full of grace, the Lord is with thee: blessed art thou among women. Who having heard, was troubled at his saying, and thought with herself what manner of salutation this should be. And the angel said to her: Fear not, Mary, for thou hast found grace with God.

Behold thou shalt conceive in thy womb, and shalt bring forth a son; and thou shalt call his name Jesus. He shall be great, and shall be called the Son of the most High; and the Lord God shall give unto him the throne of David his father; and he shall reign in the house of Jacob for ever. And of his kingdom there shall be no end. And Mary said to the angel: How shall this be done, because I know not man? And the angel answering, said to her: The Holy Ghost shall come upon thee, and the power of the most High shall overshadow thee. And therefore also the Holy which shall be born of thee shall be called the Son of God.

And behold thy cousin Elizabeth, she also hath conceived a son in her old age; and this is the sixth month with her that is called barren: Because no word shall be impossible with God. And Mary said: Behold the

---

[53] Kaczmarek, *Mary and the Power of God's Love*, 135.

handmaid of the Lord; be it done to me according to thy word. And the angel departed from her.[54]

Vittorio Matteo Corcos. *Annunciazione.* 1904.

---

[54] Luke 1:26-38.

Carl Heinrich Bloch. *The Annunciation.* Circa 1890.

Ludovico Carracci. *Annunciation.* 1603-1604.

St. Alphonsus Liguori

O most humble Mary, thou by this thy humility didst so enamour thy God that thou didst draw Him to thee, so as to become thy Son and our Redeemer.[55]

The Visitation

And Mary rising up in those days, went into the hill country with haste into a city of Juda. And she entered into the house of Zachary, and saluted Elizabeth.

And it came to pass, that when Elizabeth heard the salutation of Mary, the infant leaped in her womb. And Elizabeth was filled with the Holy Ghost: And she cried out with a loud voice, and said: Blessed art thou among women, and blessed is the fruit of thy womb. And whence is this to me, that the mother of my Lord should come to me? For behold as soon as the voice of thy salutation sounded in my ears, the infant in my womb leaped for joy. And blessed art thou that hast believed, because those things shall be accomplished that were spoken to thee by the Lord.

And Mary said: My soul doth magnify the Lord. And my spirit hath rejoiced in God my Saviour. Because he hath regarded the humility of his handmaid; for behold from henceforth all generations shall call me blessed. Because he that is mighty, hath done great things to me; and holy is his name. And his mercy is from generation unto generations, to them that fear him.

He hath shewed might in his arm: he hath scattered the proud in the conceit of their heart. He hath put down the mighty from their seat, and hath exalted the humble. He hath filled the hungry with good things; and the rich he hath sent empty away. He hath received Israel his servant, being

---

[55] Alphonsus Liguori, *The Glories of Mary* (Rockford, IL: TAN, 1977), 636.

mindful of his mercy: As he spoke to our fathers, to Abraham and to his seed forever.

And Mary abode with her about three months; and she returned to her own house.[56]

Carl Heinrich Bloch. *The Meeting of Mary and Elizabeth*. n.d.

[56] Luke 1:39-56.

St. Alphonsus Liguori

O most holy Mary, since thou dispensest so many graces to those who ask thee for them, I beseech thee to grant me thy humility. Thou esteemest thyself as nothing before God; but I am worse than nothing for I am a sinner. Thou canst make me humble; do so, for the love of that God who made thee His Mother.[57]

The Nativity

And it came to pass, that when they were there, her days were accomplished, that she should be delivered. And she brought forth her firstborn son, and wrapped him up in swaddling clothes, and laid him in a manger; because there was no room for them in the inn.

And it came to pass, after the angels departed from them into heaven, the shepherds said one to another: Let us go over to Bethlehem, and let us see this word that is come to pass, which the Lord hath shewed to us.

And they came with haste; and they found Mary and Joseph, and the infant lying in the manger. And seeing, they understood of the word that had been spoken to them concerning this child. And all that heard, wondered; and at those things that were told them by the shepherds. But Mary kept all these words, pondering them in her heart. And the shepherds returned, glorifying and praising God, for all the things they had heard and seen, as it was told unto them.[58]

---

[57] Liguori, *The Glories of Mary*, 637.
[58] Luke 2:1-20.

Paolo de Matteis. *The Adoration of the Shepherds.* 1712.

Venerable Mary of Agreda, on Jesus' Love for Mary

[Jesus spent his life] in demonstrations and tokens of such intense love [of Mary], that neither the understanding of men nor of angels was able to comprehend it.[59]

Cana

And the third day, there was a marriage in Cana of Galilee: and the mother of Jesus was there. And Jesus also was invited, and his disciples, to the marriage. And the wine failing, the mother of Jesus saith to him: They have no wine. And Jesus saith to her: Woman, what is that to me and to thee? my hour is not yet come. His mother saith to the waiters: Whatsoever he shall say to you, do ye.

Now there were set there six waterpots of stone, according to the manner of the purifying of the Jews, containing two or three measures apiece. Jesus saith to them: Fill the waterpots with water. And they filled them up to the brim. And Jesus saith to them: Draw out now, and carry to the chief steward of the feast. And they carried it. And when the chief steward had tasted the water made wine, and knew not whence it was, but the waiters knew who had drawn the water; the chief steward calleth the bridegroom, And saith to him: Every man at first setteth forth good wine, and when men have well drunk, then that which is worse. But thou hast kept the good wine until now.

This beginning of miracles did Jesus in Cana of Galilee; and manifested his glory, and his disciples believed in him. After this he went down to

---

[59] Mary of Agreda, *Divine Mysteries of the Most Holy Rosary* (Necedah, WI: J.M.J. Book, 1979), 19.

Capharnaum, he and his mother, and his brethren, and his disciples: and they remained there not many days.[60]

The Cross

Now there stood by the cross of Jesus, his mother, and his mother's sister, Mary of Cleophas, and Mary Magdalen.

When Jesus therefore had seen his mother and the disciple standing whom he loved, he saith to his mother: Woman, behold thy son. After that, he saith to the disciple: Behold thy mother. And from that hour, the disciple took her to his own. Afterwards, Jesus knowing that all things were now accomplished, that the scripture might be fulfilled, said: I thirst. Now there was a vessel set there full of vinegar. And they, putting a sponge full of vinegar and hyssop, put it to his mouth. Jesus therefore, when he had taken the vinegar, said: It is consummated. And bowing his head, he gave up the ghost.[61]

---

[60] John 2:1-12. "What is that to me," the literal translation being "What to me to thee." This is not a harsh reply, as it sounds to our modern ears that don't understand ancient Jewish idioms. This phrase is in fact one of tremendous deference, the same phrase used by demons when confronted by Jesus (cf. Mark 1:24). At Cana, Jesus is *deferring* to His Mother, and Jesus knows when Mary speaks the Holy Spirit is speaking through her. As the Holy Spirit led Jesus into the wilderness for His forty days fast and combat with the devil, so here the Holy Spirit through Mary is leading Jesus to begin His public ministry. When Jesus says that His "hour" has not yet come, in John's terminology this means the Cross—in other words, "Mother, this means the road to the Cross begins—you are the Woman, the New Eve, who will now crush the devil's head, offering me to death on the Cross." Mary also knows what Jesus is going to do at Cana (cf. the Douay Rheims Bible commentary on this passage)—she knew the miracle He was going to perform, but Jesus wanted it to be through her intercession and He wanted to go to the Cross by her consent, the New Eve leading the New Adam to lay down His life—the opposite of Eve leading Adam to sin.
[61] John 19:25-30.

Mary to St. Brigid of Sweden

And when He looked down at me from the Cross, and I looked up at Him, tears streamed from my eyes like blood from veins. And when He saw me so overwhelmed with grief, my sorrow made Him suffer so much that all the pains which He felt from His wounds were surpassed by the sight of the grief in which He beheld me. Therefore I boldly assert that His suffering became my suffering because His Heart was mine. And just as Adam and Eve sold the world for an apple, so in a certain sense my Son and I redeemed the world with one Heart.[62]

---

[62] Brown, *The Life of Mary*, 214.

William-Adolphe Bouguereau. *Christ Meeting His Mother on the Way to Calvary.* 1888.

Bartolomé Esteban Perez Murillo. *Our Lady of Sorrows.* 1668.

Mary's Assumption, Mary to Venerable Mary of Agreda

Later, after the funeral, the Lord descended in a dazzling beam of light to the tomb of the Blessed Virgin, accompanied by Mary's soul and by innumerable angels. Then the holy soul of the Mother of God penetrated into her body in the sepulcher, reanimated it, and rose up again united to it, utterly radiant, gloriously attired, and indescribably beautiful...the whole universe seemed to chant exultantly: 'Who is this that cometh up from the desert, flowing with delights, leaning upon her Beloved?'...she was attired in a marvelous sparkling robe that trailed behind her and scintillated with multicolored iridescence...Then the three divine Persons solemnly placed on Mary's bowed head a splendid gleaming crown of glory which far exceeds in beauty any crown that ever has been or ever will be awarded to a creature by God... 'Our Beloved and Chosen One among creatures, Our Kingdom is yours. You are the Queen...Our will shall ever be ready to accomplish your will...You shall be the Friend and Defender of the just and of Our friends. All of them shall you comfort, console, and fill with blessings according to their devotion to you... For we wish nothing to be given to the world that does not pass through your hands.'[63]

---

[63] Brown, *The Life of Mary*, 255-257.

Bartolomé Esteban Perez Murillo. *The Assumption of the Virgin.* 1670.

Revelation

And a great sign appeared in heaven: A woman clothed with the sun, and the moon under her feet, and on her head a crown of twelve stars.[64]

Francesco Vanni. *Immacolata Concezione con Gesù Bambino e Dio Padre.* 1588.

_____

[64] Revelation 12:1.

Pellevoisin, Apparition of Mary to Estelle Faguette

His [Jesus's] Heart is so full of love for My Heart, that He can never refuse me anything.[65]

Pompeo Batoni. *Sacra Famiglia.* 1763.

---

[65] "The Messages of Pellevoisin," 7th apparition, at The Miracle Hunter, at http://www.miraclehunter.com.

II

Our Love Letter to Mary

~ After the love which we owe Jesus Christ, we must give the chief place in
our heart to the love of His Mother Mary ~
–St. Alphonsus Liguori

St. Albert the Great

"Oh, how sweet is Mary's image! See, what care artists take to make it surpass in beauty those of other saints. See how solicitous are the faithful to show it due veneration. Churches are adorned with her pictures that our thoughts may dwell devoutly on her. In heaven we shall behold not her image in marble or on canvas, but her own most beautiful soul and body. We shall gaze on her sweet countenance, and its beauty shall ravish us throughout eternity."[66]

"If a maiden, her arms laden with beautiful flowers, would beckon us to her side, how willingly we would follow the summons: if a queen bade us approach, we would probably do so with some hesitation. But behold, the Queen of virgins, the Queen of queens calls us, and we heed not her words. Strange inconsistency!"[67]

---

[66] Kevin Vost, *St. Albert the Great: Champion of Faith & Reason* (Charlotte, NC: TAN, 2011), 115.
[67] Vost, *St. Albert the Great*, 115.

St. Alphonsus Liguori

"Let them love her as much as they will, Mary is always amongst the lovers the most loving."[68]

[Jesus to St. John the Apostle] "John, if thou lovest me, love her; for thou wilt be beloved by Me in proportion to thy love for her."[69]

"Let us love her as Blessed Hermann loved her. He called her the spouse of his love… as did St. Bonaventure: 'Hail, my Lady, my Mother; nay, even my heart, my soul!'…as St. Bernard, who called her ravisher of hearts…like St. Bernardine of Sienna, who daily went to visit a devotional picture of Mary, and there declared his love [saying] he went to visit his beloved…Let us love as much as St. Francis Solano did, who, maddened as it were (but with a holy madness), with love for Mary, would sing before her picture, and accompany himself on a musical instrument, saying, that like worldly lovers, he serenaded his most sweet Queen."[70]

"O Lady, O ravisher of hearts! I will exclaim with St. Bonaventure: 'Lady, who with the love and favor thou showest thy servants dost ravish their hearts, ravish also my miserable heart, which desires ardently to love thee. Thou, my Mother, hast enamoured a God with thy beauty, and drawn Him from heaven into thy chaste womb; and shall I live without thee? No, I will never rest until I am certain of having obtained thy love; but a constant and tender love toward thee, my Mother, who hast loved me with so much tenderness,' even when I was ungrateful toward thee. And what should I now be, O Mary, if thou hadst not obtained so many mercies for me? Since, then, thou didst love me so much when I loved thee not, how much more may I not now hope from thee, now that I love thee? I love thee, O my Mother, and I would that I had a heart to love thee in place of all those unfortunate creatures who love thee not. I would that I could speak with a

---

[68] Liguori, *The Glories of Mary*, 38.
[69] Liguori, *The Glories of Mary*, 130.
[70] Liguori, *The Glories of Mary*, 38-39.

thousand tongues, that all might know thy greatness, thy holiness, thy mercy, and the love with which thou lovest all who love thee. Had I riches, I would employ them all for thy honor. Had I subjects, I would make them all thy lovers. In fine, if the occasion presented itself I would lay down my life for thy glory. I love thee, then, O my Mother; but at the same time I fear that I do not love thee as I ought; for I hear that love makes lovers like the person loved. If, then, I see myself so unlike thee, it is a mark that I do not love thee. Thou art so pure, and I defiled with many sins; thou so humble, and I so proud; thou so holy, and I so wicked. This, then, is what thou hast to do, O Mary: since thou lovest me, make me like thee. Thou hast all power to change hearts; take, then, mine and change it. Show the world what thou canst do for those who love thee. Make me a saint; make me thy worthy child. This is my hope."[71]

"In fine, O sovereign Princess, from the immense ocean of thy beauty the beauty and grace of all creatures flowed forth as rivers. The sea learnt to curls its waves, and to wave its crystal waters from the golden hair which gracefully floated over thy shoulders and ivory neck. The crystal fountains and their transparent depths learnt their tranquil and steady flow from the serenity of thy beautiful brow and placid countenance. The lovely rainbow, when in full beauty, learnt with studious care its graceful bend from thy eyebrows, thus better to send forth its rays of light. The morning star itself, and the sweet stars at night, are sparks from thy beautiful eyes. The white lilies and ruby roses stole their colors from thy lovely cheeks. Envious purple and coral sigh for the color of thy lips. The most delicious milk and sweetest honey are distillations from the sweet honeycomb of thy mouth. The scented jasmine and fragrant Damasc rose stole their perfume from thy breath. The loftiest cedar and the most erect, the fairest cypress, were happy when they beheld their image in thy erect and lofty neck. The palm-tree,

---

[71] Liguori, *The Glories of Mary*, 43-44.

emulous and jealous, likened itself to thy noble stature. In fine, O Lady, every created beauty is a shadow and trace of thy beauty."[72]

Anton van Dyck. *The Vision of the Blessed Hermann Joseph.* 1629-1630.

---

[72] Liguori, *The Glories of Mary*, 667-668.

Sandro Botticelli. *Madonna del Magnificat.* 1481.

"O Mother of sinners, under whose mantle we are defended; O consolation of the world, in which all who are afflicted, infirm, and disconsolate, find consolation; O beautiful eyes, which steal hearts; O coral lips, which imprison souls; O generous hands, filled with lilies, and which always distribute graces; O pure creature, who appearest a God, and whom I should have taken for God, had not faith taught me that thou art not so, although thou hast a splendor, and I know not what of divine sovereignty…O Mary, Mary more beautiful than all creatures, lovely after Jesus above all loves, more dear than all created things, gracious above every grace, pity this miserable heart of mine; miserable because it does not love thee; and it ought to love thee. Thou canst inflame it with thy holy love. Turn O Mary, thy loving eyes upon me; look at me, and draw me to thee; and grant that after God I may love no other but thee, most gracious, most amiable Mary, Mother of Jesus, and my Mother."[73]

Angelico Chavez (20th Century)

"Mary"

Miriam, Mary, Maria, Marie,
What voweled jewel might this be?

Is it a sapphire love,
Of purest water true?
Or is it water of
A sapphire hue?

Miriam, Marie, Maria, Mary
So crystal-cut, yet limpid, airy!

It flows in regal tones,
Glitters like both of these:
The sea-reflecting stones,
The jeweled seas.

Mary, Marie, Maria, Miriam,
Ocean of beryl, sea-lit beryllium!

Gem for the Father's ring,

---

[73] Liguori, *The Glories of Mary*, 669-670.

Stone of the Son's great crown,
Glint on the Spirit's wing,
Light pouring down.

Miriam, Mary, Marie, Maria,
Pendant for my lips, Maria![74]

Servant of God Fr. Anselm Treves

"Would that I had billions of lives in order to live them all at the feet of Mary, billions of hearts in order to love her mightily."[75]

St. Bernadette

"What I can assure you of is that she is real and alive, that she moves, smiles and speaks just like us...I've never seen anything so beautiful...so lovely that, when you have seen her once, you would willingly die to see her again."[76]

"Once one sees Mary, he wants no more of this world."[77]

---

[74] M. Therese, *I Sing of a Maiden: The Mary Book of Verse* (New York: Macmillan, 1947), 344.

[75] Stefano Manelli, *Devotion to Our Lady* (New Bedford, MA: Academy of the Immaculate, 2001), 16.

[76] Francois Trochu, *Saint Bernadette Soubirous* (Charlotte, NC: TAN, 2012), 45.

[77] Manelli, *Devotion to Our Lady*, 43.

Domenico Tojetti. *At Sacred Spring* (detail). 1877.

St. Bernard of Clairvaux

"Most worthy of being crowned with a diadem of stars is that august head which, surpassing in splendor all the stars of the firmament, is more an ornament to them than they are to it. And what wonder that she who is clothed with the sun should be crowned with the stars? She is encompassed 'as with the flowers of roses in the days of the spring' (Ecclus. 1. 8) and as with the lilies of the valleys. For the Bridegroom's 'left hand is under her head and with His right He embraces her' (Cant. Ii. 6). Who can appraise the jewels that adorn Mary's crown? Who can name the stars that compose her queenly diadem? My brethren, it is beyond the power of any man to say what is the nature of this crown and rightly to explain its constitution."[78]

"Remember, O most gracious Virgin Mary,
that never was it known that anyone who fled to thy protection,
implored thy help, or sought thy intercession
was left unaided.
Inspired by this confidence,
I fly unto thee, O Virgin of virgins, my Mother.
To thee do I come, before thee I stand, sinful and sorrowful.
O Mother of the Word Incarnate,
despise not my petitions,
but in thy mercy, hear and answer me.
Amen."

---

[78] St. Bernard of Clairvaux, *St. Bernard's Sermons on the Blessed Virgin Mary* (Chulmleigh, Devon: Augustine, 1987), 214.

Pascal Adolphe Jean Dagnan Bouveret. *Consolatrix Afflictorum.* 1903.

St. Bernardine of Sienna

"…my lady friend is so beautiful that I've fallen head over heels in love with her! She lives just outside the Camollia gate. And I have to see her at least once a day—otherwise I can't sleep at night…I have fallen in love with the Blessed Virgin Mary, Mother of God, to whom I have been devoted since my childhood and in whom I have placed all my hopes. It is she whom I love so intensely, whom I seek, and whom I yearn to see…Yes, my 'lady love' and my hope is the Virgin Mother of God!"[79]

Bob Lord

"My relationship with Mary is a very personal one. She is my first love. I can talk to Mary. I can count on her. I have been in love with her for as long as I can remember. It's been an on again, off again romance with us, not on her part, but on mine. She's constant. She has always 'been'…I always came back. She was always there…I love you. I have always loved you…I deeply love Mary. I always have. I put her on a pedestal, not the way you would a holy person, or a saint, but like the perfect woman whom you've found, and will love forever. I want to shout it from the rooftops. 'I LOVE HER! I'M IN LOVE WITH MARY!!'"[80]

St. Bonaventure

"To say that you are my Mother is next to nothing; oh Mary, you are my absolute love!"[81]

"One should be ready to defend Mary's privileges even at the risk of his life."[82]

"It is the privilege of the glory of Mary, that after God, our greatest happiness is from her" (De Laud. Virg.).[83]

"As a field is full of the scents of various flowers, so is Mary full of the fair fame of fragrant sprinkling. Of her fullness we may understand what we

---

[79] Raphael Brown, *Saints Who Saw Mary* (Charlotte, NC: TAN, 2012), 78-79.
[80] Bob and Penny Lord, *The Many Faces of Mary, A Love Story* (Journeys of Faith, 1987), 11-12.
[81] Manelli, *Devotion to Our Lady*, 9.
[82] Manelli, *Devotion to Our Lady*, 13.
[83] D. Roberto, *The Love of Mary* (Rockford, IL: TAN, 1984), 100.

read in Genesis: 'Behold the smell of my son is the smell of a full field, which God hath blessed" (Gen. XXVII, 27). This field is Mary, in whom the treasure of the angels, yea verily, the whole treasure of God the Father is hidden. Happy is he 'who sells all that he has, and buys that field.' The full odor of this full field is the full fair fame of Mary, her full honor. Of this St. Jerome saith: 'Because she was filled with the many odors of the virtues, there came forth from her a most sweet odor, rejoicing the angelic spirits.' Of this odor she herself, glorying, could use the words of Ecclesiasticus (XXIV, 20): 'I gave a sweet smell like cinnamon and aromatical balm.'"[84]

"But behold Mary, the Spouse of the Holy Spirit, as she is and was most beautiful in conversation, so also is she most sweet in her address, as it is said in the Canticle of Canticles: 'As a dropping honeycomb,' etc. Oh, what honey-flowing words have those sweet lips of Mary often distilled! Had she not indeed milk and honey under her tongue in those two sweet words which she addressed to Gabriel? Had not Mary milk upon her tongue when she said: 'How shall this be done, for I know not man?' (Luke I, 34). Had she not honey on her tongue when she uttered that honey-sweet word: 'Behold the handmaid of the Lord, be it done unto me according to thy word'? From the sweetness of this word, throughout the whole world, the Heavens have dropped honey. Mary had honey on her tongue in her eloquent words to God; she had milk on her tongue in her agreeable speech to her neighbor. Of how great sweetness and beauty is that Spouse of the Supreme Consoler! Because, as St. Augustine says, 'Who is this virgin, so holy that the Holy Spirit deigns to come to her? So beautiful, that God chooses her for His Spouse?'"[85]

[84] Bonaventure, *The Mirror of the Blessed Virgin Mary*, at EWTN, www.ewtn.com, Chapter VII.

[85] Bonaventure, *The Mirror of the Blessed Virgin Mary*, Chapter X.

Psalter of the Blessed Virgin Mary (Selected Psalms)
Psalm I

Blessed is the man, O Virgin Mary,
who loves thy name;
thy grace will comfort his soul.

He will be refreshed as by fountains of water;
thou wilt produce in him the fruits of justice.

Blessed are thou among women;
by the faith of thy holy heart.

By the beauty of thy body thou surpasses all women;
by the excellence of thy sanctity
thou surpassest all angels and archangels.

Thy mercy and thy grace are preached everywhere;
God has blessed the works of thy hands.

Psalm XI

Save me, O Mother of fair love:
fount of clemency and sweetness of piety.

Thou alone makest the circuit of the earth;
that thou mayest help those that call upon thee.

Beautiful are thy ways;
and thy paths are peaceful.

In thee shine forth the beauty of chastity,
the light of justice,
and the splendor of truth.

Thou art clothed with the sunrays as with a vesture:
resplendent with a shining twelve-starred crown.

Psalm XVIII

The heavens declare thy glory;
and the fragrance of thy unguents is spread abroad
among the nations.

Sing unto her, ye lost sinners:
and she will rain down upon you the grace of her sweetness.

Glorify her, ye just, before the throne of God:
for by the fruit of her womb you have worked justice.
Praise ye her, ye heaven of heavens:
and the whole earth will glorify her name.

Psalm LVIII

Deliver me from mine enemies, O Lady of the world:
arise to meet me, O Queen of piety.

The purest gold is thy ornament:
the sardine stone and the topaz are thy diadem.

The jasper and the amethyst are in thy right hand:
the beryl and the chrysolite in thy left.

The hyacinths are on thy breast;
shining carbuncles are the jewels of thy bracelets.

Myrrh, frankincense, and balsam are on thy hands:
The sapphire and the emerald on thy fingers.[86]

Boston Catholic Journal

[While the *Little Office of the Blessed Virgin Mary* is mentioned here, love for Mary is the central point, and further, one can easily replace that part of the text with "the Rosary", the daily prayer to Mary that most pray. The Rosary is also the most powerful means, after the Mass, of being intimately united with her.]

"First, a Note to Men:

Praying the *Little Office of the Blessed Virgin Mary* is very much a manly aspiration to devout Catholic men, as it is a womanly aspiration to devout Catholic women. Devotion to Mary throughout history has been the hallmark of a devout and manly Catholic unafraid to express his love for, his commitment to — and his defense of — Mary Most Holy. Mary needs, Our Lady calls to, her Josephs in this world.

All those women who walk in the footprints of the Mother of God bring to her, in prayer, and through this Office, their magnificent womanhood and all that is beautifully inseparable from it — especially the nurturing of *that life created anew in Christ*, both in themselves and in others to whom they, in turn, are called to be *other* Mary's in this world, bringing the sons and daughters of men to Christ, her Son.

Men, in turn, bring their strength, their unwavering and courageous commitment, to the service of Mary — even to the *protection* of Mary, as befits, even compels, every man in his devotion to whom he loves — and

---

[86] M. Therese, *I Sing of a Maiden*, 57-59.

most especially in his love for the Mother of God ... who deigned to love him first!

Countless male Saints of the Church were dedicated and totally bound to Mary in love! Indeed, the place of Mary in the life of a Priest and that of any Catholic Christian man should be an integral part of their spiritual lives as Catholics. There is no doubt whatever, as we see so clearly throughout the history of the Church, that men — priests and lay alike — who are devoted to Mary possess and live their Faith passionately, manfully, fearlessly, in a way conspicuously absent in men without devotion to Mary. They behold in Mary not only Mother but Queen: *Regina Angelorum, Regina Apostolorum*, to whom they joyfully submit their lives in loving service and uncompromising faithfulness.

Mary, Mother of God as she is, still needs her guardians and protectors, she needs that fearless witness to humility, to simplicity and to trust through manly men being willing, even eager, to be seen and known as those fighting for her Son's glorious cause, for the triumph of good over evil, life over death, Christ over the world!...

... Being faithful to keeping the time and making the effort to pray the daily Office, or some part of that Office, takes perseverance and discipline, a perseverance that can only be motivated by love and a discipline that manifests itself in sacrifice; it is the courtly *invitation to the soul of a man to bring honor to his Lady and Queen* and to the Church whose image she is.

Mary needs her Josephs! May this be a call to men, this call to enter into, and to pray, the *Little Office*, and honor her who is so worthy of honor."[87]

---

[87] Boston Catholic Journal, "The Little Office of the Blessed Virgin Mary," at Boston Catholic Journal, at www.boston-catholic-journal.com.

William Adolphe Bouguereau. *Song of the Angels.* 1881.

Dante Alighieri

The Divine Comedy: Paradiso, Canto XXXI-XXXIII
'...look up unto the circles, to the highest
until your eyes behold, enthroned, the Queen
who holds as subject this devoted realm.'

And there, smiling, upon their games and song
I saw a beauty that reflected bliss
within the eyes of all the other saints;

and even if I were as rich as words
as in remembering, I would not dare
describe the least part of such beauty's bliss.

'Now look at that face which resembles Christ
the most, for only in its radiance
will you be made ready to look at Christ.'

I saw such bliss rain down upon her face,
bestowed on it by all those sacred minds
created to fly through those holy heights,

that of all things I witnessed to this point
nothing had held me more spellbound than this,
nor shown a greater likeness unto God...

'Oh Virgin Mother, daughter of your son,
most humble, most exalted of all creatures
chosen of God in His eternal plan,

you are the one who ennobled human nature
to the extent that He did not disdain,
Who was its Maker, to make Himself man.

Within your womb rekindled was the love
that gave the warmth that did allow this flower
to come to bloom within this timeless peace.

For all up here you are the noonday torch
of charity, and down on earth, for men,
the living spring of their eternal hope.

Lady, you are so great, so powerful
that who seeks grace without recourse to you
would have his wish fly upward without wings.

Not only does your loving kindness rush
to those who ask for it, but often times
it flows spontaneously before the plea.

In you is tenderness, in you is pity,
in you is munificence—in you unites
all that is good in God's created beings.'

Those eyes so loved and reverenced by God,
now fixed on him who prayed, made clear to us
how precious true devotion is to her;

then she looked into the Eternal Light,
into whose being, we must believe, no eyes

of other creatures pierce with such insight.[88]

D. Roberto

"I now no longer wonder that they who know thee, Most Amiable Mary, are transported with love for thee; St. Bernardine of Sienna called thee his Beloved; Saint Philip Neri, his Delight…Blessed Herman, his Beloved Spouse; Saint Bonaventure his Heart and his Soul; Saint Bernard, Captivator of Hearts…"[89]

"God applied Himself more in forming that single body of His Most Holy Mother, than all the celestial and sublunary orbs, and all that is in them. With this measure, imagine, if you can, with what proportion and symmetry of parts, with what beauty of color, with what pleasure corresponding to the five senses, God formed that sacred and beautiful body, which was to be the companion and coadjutor of the most beautiful soul, except that of Christ, that ever has proceeded or will proceed from the hands of God; that body, which was to captivate the hearts of men with its comeliness, its amiability, its love; that body, finally, which was to form in its time the body of a God made man, who was 'beautiful above the sons of men.' And in fact, says Albertus Magnus (Super Missus est), as Our Lord Jesus Christ was the most beautiful among the sons of men, so the Blessed Virgin was beautiful and fair above all the daughters of Adam. She had the highest and most perfect degree of beauty that can be found in a human body, after that of her Son; and Denis the Carthusian (Lib. i. art. 2 and 36), citing the same Albertus Magnus, asserts that as the humanity of the Redeemer was most beautiful by its union with the Word, so the Mother was beautiful as the most closely connected with this divine union, and that

---

[88] Dante Alighieri, Trans. Mark Musa, *Paradise* (New York: Penguin, 1984), 365-391.

[89] Roberto, *The Love of Mary*, 213.

her appearance was illustrated by a certain splendor, and her virginal flesh gave forth a most sweet odor.

It is not for us to say with how great and beautiful gifts God adorned this His Incorruptible Tabernacle, chosen from eternity. He alone knows this. Richard of Saint Laurence says: 'How great is the beauty of Mary, He only knows who gave this beauty; it is seen by the Creator, but is known to no creature. And because He alone knows it, He only can make its description and encomium,' as when Saint Bridget heard Him address His Mother: 'Thy beauty surpasses the beauty of the angels and of all created things' (Lib. Revelat. c. 16).

But who can ever tell, or in any manner express, the beauty which Mary possesses now that she reigns glorious and immortal in Heaven, making even paradise more blessed? The beauty of Mary did not endure for a few years only, like that of all the other children of Adam, which soon languishes and withers like a flower, and terminates in the corruption and deformity of a corpse. No; that Most Holy Tabernacle of the Divinity, that Sacred Ark of the True Testament, was not to be made subject to corruption. The tabernacle and the ark of the Old Testament were made of the incorruptible wood of Setim, though only destined to keep the tables of the law; but those of the New Testament were to hold the Lawgiver, the Author of Immortality.

Immortal, then, was the beauty of this Most Beautiful Empress of the World; for after she had reached the thirty-third year of her age, at which period the human body arrives at its natural perfection, no change or decline was perceived in her; but she remained, as long as she lived, in that same state of perfection, so proportioned and beautiful, that she was a wonder not only to human nature, but even to the angels."[90]

"And such is the beauty of the Most Holy Virgin in Heaven, that according to the common opinion of the Doctors, she would suffice to

---

[90] Roberto, *The Love of Mary*, 98-99.

constitute a paradise by herself alone, and to make all those spirits and fortunate souls blessed."[91]

St. Dominic Savio

"Oh my Mother, I want always to be your little child. Obtain for me that I may die rather than commit a sin against the virtue of modesty."[92]

[To a companion who wondered why he usually kept his eyes downcast rather than looking about] "I want to keep my eyes pure to behold Our Lady in Paradise."[93]

---

[91] Roberto, *The Love of Mary*, 100.
[92] Manelli, *Devotion to Our Lady*, 132.
[93] Manelli, *Devotion to Our Lady*, 132.

William Adolphe Bouguereau. *The Madonna of the Lilies.* 1899.

Edgar Allan Poe

"Hymn"

At morn- at noon- at twilight dim-
Maria! thou hast heard my hymn!
In joy and woe- in good and ill-
Mother of God, be with me still!
When the hours flew brightly by,
And not a cloud obscured the sky,
My soul, lest it should truant be,
Thy grace did guide to thine and thee;
Now, when storms of Fate o'ercast
Darkly my Present and my Past,
Let my Future radiant shine
With sweet hopes of thee and thine.[94]

Fernande Voisin, Apparition of Beauraing, Belgium (November 1932 and January 1933)

[A conversation between Mary and Fernande Voisin, 15, one of the five children who saw Mary]

"Do you love my Son?"
"Yes!" the girl exclaimed.
"Do you love me?"
"Oh, yes!"
"Then sacrifice yourself for me."[95]

---

[94] Edgar Allan Poe, "Hymn," at https://ebooks.adelaide.edu.au.
[95] Pierced Hearts, "Apparition of the Virgin Mary in Beauraing, Belgium," at *Servants of the Pierced Hearts of Jesus and Mary*, at www.piercedhearts.org.

St. Francis of Assisi

A Salutation to the Blessed Virgin Mary

Hail Lady, Holy Queen, Holy Mary Theotokos, who art the Virgin made church and the One elect by the Most Holy Father of Heaven, whom He consecrated with His Most Holy beloved Son and with the Holy Spirit, the Paraclete; Thou in whom was and is all fulness of grace and every good.

Hail His Palace;
Hail His Tabernacle;
Hail His Home.
Hail His Vestment;
Hail His Handmaid;
Hail His Mother;

And hail all you holy virtues, which through the grace and illumination of the Holy Spirit are infused into the hearts of the faithful, so that from those unfaithful you make them faithful to God.
Amen.[96]

Francis Thompson

"The After Woman"
Daughter of the ancient Eve,
We know the gifts ye gave--and give.
Who knows the gifts which YOU shall give,
Daughter of the newer Eve?
You, if my soul be augur, you

---

[96] Francis of Assisi, "A Salutation to the Blessed Virgin Mary," at Franciscan Archive, at http://franciscan-archive.org/franciscana/prayers.html.

Shall--O what shall you not, Sweet, do?
The celestial traitress play,
And all mankind to bliss betray;
With sacrosanct cajoleries
And starry treachery of your eyes,
Tempt us back to Paradise!
Make heavenly trespass;--ay, press in
Where faint the fledge-foot seraphin,
Blest Fool! Be ensign of our wars,
And shame us all to warriors!
Unbanner your bright locks,--advance
Girl, their gilded puissance,
I' the mystic vaward, and draw on
After the lovely gonfalon
Us to out-folly the excess
Of your sweet foolhardiness;
To adventure like intense
Assault against Omnipotence!

Give me song, as She is, new,
Earth should turn in time thereto!
New, and new, and thrice so new,
All old sweets, New Sweet, meant you!
Fair, I had a dream of thee,
When my young heart beat prophecy,
And in apparition elate
Thy little breasts knew wax-ed great,
Sister of the Canticle,
And thee for God grown marriageable.
How my desire desired your day,
That, wheeled in rumour on its way,

Shook me thus with presentience! Then
Eden's lopped tree shall shoot again:
For who Christ's eyes shall miss, with those
Eyes for evident nuncios?
Or who be tardy to His call
In your accents augural?

Who shall not feel the Heavens hid
Impend, at tremble of your lid,
And divine advent shine avowed
Under that dim and lucid cloud;
Yea, 'fore the silver apocalypse
Fail, at the unsealing of your lips?
When to love YOU is (O Christ's Spouse!)
To love the beauty of His house;
Then come the Isaian days; the old
Shall dream; and our young men behold
Vision--yea, the vision of Thabor mount,
Which none to other shall recount,
Because in all men's hearts shall be
The seeing and the prophecy.
For ended is the Mystery Play,
When Christ is life, and you the way;
When Egypt's spoils are Israel's right,
And Day fulfils the married arms of Night.
But here my lips are still.
Until

You and the hour shall be revealed,
This song is sung and sung not, and its words are sealed.[97]

Franz Werfel

[In his most famous book, *The Song of Bernadette*, Franz Werfel penned incredibly beautiful descriptions of Mary at Lourdes, at the same time capturing St. Bernadette's love for Mary and Mary's love for St. Bernadette. The following passages, woven from some of Werfel's descriptions of the several appearances of Mary to St. Bernadette, form a wonderfully sweet portrait of Mary's beauty, Mary's love for each of us, and St. Bernadette's love for Mary.]

"And this someone is not at all an unprecise and ghostly or a transparent and airy image, no changeful dream vision, but a very young lady, delicate and dainty, visibly of flesh and blood, short rather than tall, for she stands calmly and without touching the side or arch in the narrow oval of the niche…her easy snow-white raiment is so cut as to indicate her delicate waistline. Bernadette had had a chance recently to witness the church wedding of the youngest daughter of the Lafites, and the raiment of the lady was best comparable to that of a distinguished bride. For there is first the loose and precious cloak of veiling that reaches from the head to the ankles. Yet, charmingly enough, the small bridal lady seems not to wear the fashionable high coiffure, curled with irons and held by tortoise-shell combs, that would suit her rank. Wavy ringlets of her light brown hair escape from under the veil. A quite broad blue girdle, lightly knotted under the breast, falls down over the knee. But what a blue! Lovely to the point of pain…what manner of fabric the white gown was made…it gleams like satin or silk; sometimes it is duller, like some unknown, very delicate, ineffably

---

[97] Thompson, "The After Woman," in *The Works of Francis Thompson, Poems: Volume II* (NY: Charles Scribner's Sons, 1913), 64.

60

snowy velvet; again it seems like a transparently thin batiste that transmits to its folds every stirring of the limbs.[98]

The lady smiles contentedly. This smile is but a deeper radiation of her graciousness. Bernadette thereupon uses the awkward gesture common to the schoolgirls of Lourdes when they meet a teaching sister of Father Pomian or His Reverence Peyramale on the street. The lady hastens to return the greeting, by far not so condescendingly as the persons in authority here named but with an air of free comradeliness. She nods repeatedly and her smile grows still brighter. This greeting creates a new situation. The web of the relationship between the two is being woven. Between these two, the blessed and the blessing one, arises and flows back and forth a stream of happiest sympathy, of immemorial unitedness, indeed the awareness of a very special solidarity that stirs the heart's core.[99]

If ever one moved to and fro in the grotto, or, still worse, turned one's back, an expression of nervous suffering would tarnish the radiance of her [Mary's] countenance. If, on the other hand, one did a painful thing— Bernadette knew this well—such as sliding on one's knees over the jagged rubble toward the rock, then she was transfigured with joy. These matters were in all likelihood allied to that word which several times the lady had whispered as if to herself, the word 'penitence.'[100]

[Bernadette] begins the first decade of Aves…At the end of each Ave [Mary] lets a pearl glide between her index finger and her thumb. But she always waits and lets Bernadette drop her little black bead first. Only when

---

[98] Franze Werfel, *The Song of Bernadette* (San Francisco: Ignatius, 2006), 53-54.

[99] Werfel, *The Song of Bernadette*, 56.

[100] Werfel, *The Song of Bernadette*, 199-200. Mary's happiness here is one of joy because when given penances, sacrifices, and mortifications Mary uses them to save souls. She takes one's little seeds, so to speak, freely given to her out of self-sacrificial love, and with them she brings new life, hence her great joy, both over the saved souls and that some reparation has been made to God for sin; selflessness is love and from it comes salvation, for oneself and others, whereas selfishness is sin and causes immense destruction and loss of souls.

the decade is finished and followed by the invocation 'Glory be to the Father and to the Son and to the Holy Spirit', does a strong breathing pass through the lady's form and does her mouth silently repeat the words…[101]

The rosary had come to be the most enchanting part of her communion. It was a tranquil-blended lostness to the world when Bernadette murmured her Ave and dropped a black bead of her poor little string and when the lady with speechless lips but clear observing eyes imitated the girl's gesture and let another pearl of her long radiant rosary glide through her fingers. That meant more than prayer in common; it was a heart-intoxicating form of contact, such as befitted a love like this. For it was then as though each of the two held an end of the same invisible staff, through the substance of which flooded back and forth between them warmth as of blood and yearnings of the soul. All objects that Bernadette touched at the lady's bidding had a new and fresh and pristine significance as if they had only now come into being, even her old, shabby rosary.[102]

In soft folds the snow-white mysterious velvet clung to the delicate limbs. The transparent veil fell from the shoulders. It rejoiced the heart to see today's mild wind toying with it. The lady seemed to be eternally a bride and for ever as such before the altar, never doffing her bridal veil…[103]

…the lady…a creature all youth, all floating dainty maidenhood. Today the lady harbored in her heart no aims beyond those whereby the isolation of these two in their love could be diminished. Today for the first time was the full and undivided love of her who brought such bliss turned wholly toward her who needed to absorb it. Never yet had the bridal veil fluttered so merrily in the wind; never had the brown ringlets escaped so freely from beneath the veil's border; never had the eyes been of a blue so crystalline nor ever had the half-open mouth been so ravishingly curved. Nor yet had the white fabric of the dress or the blue of the girdle been so breathtakingly

[101] Werfel, *The Song of Bernadette*, 60-61.
[102] Werfel, *The Song of Bernadette*, 263.
[103] Werfel, *The Song of Bernadette*, 105.

unheard of as on this day on which the fading sunset splendor lent them an added glow. And the smile of the lady yonder was more that of a playmate than of a great and gracious being...the lady [...] was giving her utmost. She offered and she gave herself in steady waves of drawing close and closer to the very boundary of the possible."[104]

[Shortly after the apparitions ended] Her need to be solitary was greater than ever. For to be alone was to be alone with her love, which had not been so much as touched by that farewell, but which that farewell had sweetened with continuous longing. What she felt in such hours and housed within herself of memory, and of reexperiencing—that was communicable to none and scarcely fathomed by herself."[105]

Venerable Fulton Sheen

"The mind is infinitely variable in its language, but the heart is not. The heart of a man, in the face of the woman he loves, is too poor to translate the infinity of affection into a different word. So the heart takes one expression, 'I love you,' and in saying it over and over again, it never repeats. That is what we do when we say the rosary—we are saying to God, the Trinity, to the Incarnate Son, to the Blessed Mother: 'I love you, I love you, I love you.'"[106]

"That ideal love we see beyond all creature-love, to which we instinctively turn when flesh-love fails, is the same ideal that God had in His Heart from all eternity—the Lady whom He calls 'Mother.' She is the one whom every man loves when he loves a woman—whether he knows it or not. She is what every woman wants to be when she looks at herself. She is the woman whom every man marries in ideal when he takes a spouse; she is hidden as an ideal in the discontent of every woman with the carnal

---

[104] Werfel, *The Song of Bernadette*, 355-357.
[105] Werfel, *The Song of Bernadette*, 364-365.
[106] Don Calloway, *Champions of the Rosary*, 311.

aggressiveness of man; she is the secret desire every woman has to be honored and fostered; she is the way every woman wants to command respect and love because of her goodness of body and soul. And this blueprint of love, whom God loved before the world was made, this Dream Woman before women were, is the one of whom every heart can say in its depths of depths: 'She is the woman I love!'"[107]

St. Gabriel the Archangel

"With faith the Angel adored the divine goodness which was so marked in Mary. He admired the humble girl elevated to such wondrous heights. He rejoiced at the honor of being the promulgator of the mystery of the incarnation and redemption."[108]

The Divine Comedy: Paradiso, Canto XXXII

…who is that angel who so joyously
looks straight into the eyes of Heaven's Queen,
so much in love he seems to burn like fire?"

…and he: 'All loving pride and gracious joy,
as much as soul or angel can possess,
is all in him, and we would have it so,

for he it is who bore the palm below
to Mary when the Son of God had willed
to bear the weight of man's flesh on Himself.[109]

[107] Sheen, *The World's First Love*, 24.
[108] James Alberione, *Glories and Virtues of Mary* (Boston, MA: Daughters of St. Paul, 1982), 28.
[109] Dante, *Paradise*, 379.

Carlo Dolci. *Angel of the Annunciation.* 1653.

St. Gabriel Possenti

[Of his love for Mary, St. Gabriel said] "I feel unable to tell you even one percent," and "If I had to tell everything, I would never finish."[110] [Of him, his spiritual director, Fr. Norbert, said] "It is impossible for me to describe how sincere, tender and ardent was his love for Mary, the Sorrowful Mother, and how absolutely it had taken possession of his entire heart."[111] "[He was] like dough kneaded through and through by love for Our Lady, [a love that was] so loving, active, generous, constant, resourceful, I had never seen nor heard of nor read about."[112]

"I will never refuse anything that is asked of me for love of Mary."[113]

"My heaven is the heart of my Sorrowful Mother."[114]

"The love and attachment for her that burned within Gabriel's soul found external expression in a thousand graceful acts which indicated the eagerness of his heart to be not only wholly devoted to her himself, but also to bring others to her love and service.

Hardly had he entered the novitiate when he sought to bind himself by vow to become 'Our Lady's Champion' by spreading devotion to her among the faithful. This favour was denied him at the time, but nearly five years later, after persistent pleading, he succeeded in having his desire gratified."[115]

---

[110] Gabriele Cingolani, *Saint Gabriel Possenti, Passionist: A Young Man in Love* (New York: Alaba, 2001), 101.

[111] Camillus Hollobough, *St. Gabriel, Passionist* (New York: Catholic Book Publishing, 1953), 160.

[112] Cingolani, *Saint Gabriel Possenti, Passionist*, 101.

[113] Cingolani, *Saint Gabriel Possenti, Passionist*, 104.

[114] Camillus, *St. Gabriel, Passionist*, 176.

[115] Camillus, *St. Gabriel, Passionist*, 165.

[Letter to his brother Michael Possenti, who would later marry, become a doctor, and in his old age attend the beatification and canonization of his brother Gabriel]:

"Dear Michael:

Would you have someone to love? Be it so, by all means. But whom shall you love? MARY! What creature is more beautiful, more loveable, more powerful? And do not imagine that to love, to speak and to live with Mary is wearisome and devoid of charm because she is not seen with bodily eyes. O no! The consolation, the delight of this love is so much the more pure and satisfying to the heart, as the soul is superior to the senses. Be assured, moreover, that you will meet none in this world who can make you entirely happy, for their love is inconstant or false. And were one to be found without these defects, the very thought of the parting that must come one day would fill the heart with bitterness and cruel pain. Not so with him who chooses Mary for his portion, for she is loving, faithful, constant and will never be outdone in love.

If we are in danger, she hastens to our rescue. If we are cast down she consoles us. If we are sick she comforts us. If we are in need, she runs to help us, with no thought of our past misdeeds. The moment she sees a heart that wishes to love her, she comes and reveals to it the secret of her goodness. She presses it to her bosom, she shields it, comforts it, stoops to serve it, even deigns to keep it company on its way to eternity.

When the moment of death comes, O dearest brother, think of it, when for those who love creatures all is at an end and they must go hence into the eternal abode which they have fashioned for themselves, while they cry out in despair: 'O bitter and cruel death, is it thus thou tearest me away from all I have loved'—at that hour true lovers of Mary are glad of heart. They invite death. They part without sorrow from their friends and the world, for they know that they are soon to possess the object of their love and that in her possession they will be happy for evermore."[116]

"I believe that you are the breath of Christians...In your name I find the same sweetness that St. Bernardine finds in the name of Jesus: joy in the heart, honey in the mouth, harmony to the ear...I believe that your beauty surpasses that of all men and angels..."[117]

Gautier de Coinci

"For before him came a lady, brighter than the midday sun when it is at its highest. She was dressed in a robe, all made of beaten gold, full of precious gems, so bright and glorious [that] the entire monastery shone with the light that they gave off. Her hair was more golden blonde and shimmering than fine gold; her eyes so bright they seemed like two stars. Her face [was] more resplendent than emerald or topaz. She had a roseate color so pure and fine, so delightful, so very beautiful—more so than any budding rose. Her face was so pleasing, so clear, so sweet, so lovable, whomsoever might behold himself there enough would leave all his troubles behind. She is so beautiful that in this world there is none, whatever skill he might have, who would know how to describe her at all."[118]

St. Gemma Galgani

"When will Jesus come? Tell Him that you too, Mother, want me. I want to go with you . . . I have beseeched Him for so long! You ask and Jesus would bring me very quickly to Heaven. My Mother, I desire to possess you always and I do not wish to be separated from you any longer. Oh! bring me

---

[116] Camillus, *St. Gabriel, Passionist*, 182-183.

[117] Alberione, *Glories and Virtues of Mary*, 44-45.

[118] Rachel Fulton Brown, *Mary & the Art of Prayer: The Hours of the Virgin in Medieval Christian Life and Thought* (New York: Columbia, 2018), 414-415.

to Paradise. I can live no longer without you. Do you see the suffering that you are causing me? I need your heart. Yes, each day I seek you in order to pour into this heart the sorrowful transports of mine. Do not leave me . . . O my Mother, O my Mother!"[119]

"Oh, how I love my Mother! She knows it; and then Jesus Himself gave her to me, and told me to love her so much. And what great goodness this Heavenly Mother has always shown me! What would have become of me, if I had not had her? She has always helped me in my spiritual wants; she has preserved me from countless dangers; she has freed me from the hands of the devil who was ceaselessly coming to molest me; she pleaded my cause with Jesus when I sinned, and she soothed Him when I moved Him to anger by my wicked life; she has taught me to know Him and love Him, to be good and to please Him. Ah, my dear Mother, I will love thee always and forever."[120]

Fr. Gerard Manley Hopkins

"The Blessed Virgin Compared to the Air We Breathe"
Wild air, world-mothering air,
Nestling me everywhere,
That each eyelash or hair
Girdles; goes home betwixt
The fleeciest, frailest-flixed
Snowflake; that's fairly mixed
With, riddles, and is rife
In every least thing's life;
This needful, never spent,

---

[119] Glenn Dallaire, "The Blessed Virgin Mary and St Gemma Galgani," at www.stgemmagalgani.com.
[120] Glenn Dallaire, "The Blessed Virgin Mary and St Gemma Galgani," at www.stgemmagalgani.com.

And nursing element;
My more than meat and drink,
My meal at every wink;
This air, which, by life's law,
My lung must draw and draw
Now but to breathe its praise,
Minds me in many ways
Of her who not only
Gave God's infinity
Dwindled to infancy
Welcome in womb and breast,
Birth, milk, and all the rest
But mothers each new grace
That does now reach our race—
Mary Immaculate,
Merely a woman, yet
Whose presence, power is
Great as no goddess's
Was deemèd, dreamèd; who
This one work has to do—
Let all God's glory through,
God's glory which would go
Through her and from her flow
Off, and no way but so.

I say that we are wound
With mercy round and round
As if with air: the same
Is Mary, more by name.
She, wild web, wondrous robe,
Mantles the guilty globe,

Since God has let dispense
Her prayers his providence:
Nay, more than almoner,
The sweet alms' self is her
And men are meant to share
Her life as life does air.
If I have understood,
She holds high motherhood
Towards all our ghostly good
And plays in grace her part
About man's beating heart,
Laying, like air's fine flood,
The deathdance in his blood;
Yet no part but what will
Be Christ our Saviour still.
Of her flesh he took flesh:
He does take fresh and fresh,
Though much the mystery how,
Not flesh but spirit now
And makes, O marvellous!
New Nazareths in us,
Where she shall yet conceive
Him, morning, noon, and eve;
New Bethlems, and he born
There, evening, noon, and morn—
Bethlem or Nazareth,
Men here may draw like breath
More Christ and baffle death;
Who, born so, comes to be
New self and nobler me
In each one and each one

More makes, when all is done,
Both God's and Mary's Son.
Again, look overhead
How air is azurèd;
O how! nay do but stand
Where you can lift your hand
Skywards: rich, rich it laps
Round the four fingergaps.
Yet such a sapphire-shot,
Charged, steepèd sky will not
Stain light. Yea, mark you this:
It does no prejudice.
The glass-blue days are those
When every colour glows,
Each shape and shadow shows.
Blue be it: this blue heaven
The seven or seven times seven
Hued sunbeam will transmit
Perfect, not alter it.
Or if there does some soft,
On things aloof, aloft,
Bloom breathe, that one breath more
Earth is the fairer for.
Whereas did air not make
This bath of blue and slake
His fire, the sun would shake,
A blear and blinding ball
With blackness bound, and all
The thick stars round him roll
Flashing like flecks of coal,
Quartz-fret, or sparks of salt,

In grimy vasty vault.
So God was god of old:
A mother came to mould
Those limbs like ours which are
What must make our daystar
Much dearer to mankind;
Whose glory bare would blind
Or less would win man's mind.
Through her we may see him
Made sweeter, not made dim,
And her hand leaves his light
Sifted to suit our sight.
Be thou then, O thou dear
Mother, my atmosphere;
My happier world, wherein
To wend and meet no sin;
Above me, round me lie
Fronting my froward eye
With sweet and scarless sky;
Stir in my ears, speak there
Of God's love, O live air,
Of patience, penance, prayer:
World-mothering air, air wild,
Wound with thee, in thee isled,
Fold home, fast fold thy child.[121]

---

[121] Gerard Manley Hopkins, "The Blessed Virgin Compared to the Air We Breathe," at www.bartleby.com.

St. Jacinta of Fatima

"I so love the Immaculate Heart of Mary!"[122]

"Her Heart is so good! How I love it!"[123]

"Sweet Heart of Mary, be my salvation!"[124]

"Our Lady said that her Immaculate Heart would be your refuge and your way to God. Doesn't that make you glad? I so love her Heart! It is so good!"[125]

"I so love the Immaculate Heart of Mary! It is the Heart of our Mother in heaven! Don't you find it sweet to repeat often: Heart of Mary! Sweet Heart of Mary! I have so much pleasure in it! So much pleasure!"[126]

"I'm sorry not to be able to go to Communion in reparation for the sins which offend the Immaculate Heart of Mary!"[127]

---

[122] Maria Gabriella Iannelli, "The Mediation of the Blessed Virgin Mary in the lives of Blessed Francisco and Jacinta of Fatima," in *Mary at the Foot of the Cross, VII: Acts of the Seventh International Symposium on Marian Coredemption* (New Bedford, MA: Academy of the Immaculate, 2008), 458.

[123] Iannelli, "The Mediation of the Blessed Virgin Mary".

[124] Iannelli, "The Mediation of the Blessed Virgin Mary".

[125] Chanoine Barthas and G. Da Fonseca, *Our Lady of Light* (Milwaukee: Bruce, 1948), 120.

[126] Barthas, *Our Lady of Light*, 120.

[127] Barthas, *Our Lady of Light*, 120.

The Divine Shepherdess. French Holy Card.

Charles Bosseron Chambers. *Immaculate Heart of Mary, I.* n.d.

"I love our Lord and the Blessed Virgin so much that I am never tired of telling them so."[128]

"If only I could put into all hearts what I feel here within me, what makes me love the Hearts of Jesus and Mary so!..."[129]

---

[128] Barthas, *Our Lady of Light*, 128.
[129] Barthas, *Our Lady of Light*, 130.

[After a visit of Mary to her in the hospital, not long before she died] "She added that the Blessed Virgin had looked very sad this time, and had even told her the cause of her sorrow: 'The sins which lead the greatest number of souls to perdition are the sins of the flesh. It is necessary to give up luxury, not to remain obstinately in sin, as they have done until now. Great penance is indispensable.' And Jacinta added, 'Oh! I feel so sad for our Lady! I feel so sad!'"[130]

St. John the Apostle

"He too experienced an ever-increasing love and devotion for his Master's holy Mother, and consequently he soon excelled all the others in his eagerness to honor and serve her in every possible way. John sought to be in her company as much as he could...His devotion to Mary was so evident that the other Apostles often asked John to intercede with her for them. It was because of his profound love for Mary that John earned the distinction of becoming the Beloved Disciple of Jesus..."[131]

John Joseph

"Pagan peoples have fashioned women deities and have lauded them across the millennia, yet this has been out of a misguided expression of a holy desire for union with Mary, and of that innate knowledge of Her within each heart, which has been repressed through original and personal sin. Plagued with concupiscence, men so often objectify women, and women often objectify themselves, reducing themselves to totalities to be used and adored in their own right – yet all of this, among other things, is simply a misguided expression of a desire to reverence and devote oneself to the

---

[130] Barthas, *Our Lady of Light*, 137.
[131] Brown, *The Life of Mary*, 187.

Blessed Virgin. Every heart longs for Mary, since this is indistinguishable from the thirst for God inherent in every man. Why? For God is so united to Mary in an indivisible bond of grace, that one cannot be one with God unless one is one with Mary, and vice versa."[132]

"Lady of the Snow"

There is a lady
Comely and most white,
Who in a secret cavern
Hides from the heat.

Yet when the snow falls
Out she comes to greet,
Those admirers that seek
Her face to behold.

O but few there are
Who'll stroll through snow cold
To seek that fairest white dame,
For fireplace holds.

But when she doth find
A wonderer true,
No more again is he found
For him she hides.[133]

---

[132] John Joseph, "Snow White: An Allegory of the Blessed Virgin Mary," at *Ten-Stringed Lyre of the New Israel* (22 August 2016), at http://tenstringedlyreofthenewisrael.blogspot.in/.

[133] John Joseph, "Lady of the Snow" (10 October 2015), at *Ten-Stringed Lyre of the New Israel* (22 August 2016), at http://tenstringedlyreofthenewisrael.blogspot.in/.

St. Joseph

[From interior locutions from Jesus about the life of St. Joseph to Mother Cecilia Baij, OSB, Abbess of the Benedictine Convent of St. Peter in Montefiascone, Italy, 1743-1766]

"Do I really deserve to set eyes upon this holy maiden, this marvel of grace? Oh who shall be so fortunate as to receive Her as his bride? I am really much too insignificant and unworthy to seek to acquire Her as my spouse. If I could obtain the great favor of becoming Her servant, how happy I would be!"[134]

"My God, what a great favor have You bestowed upon me, by entrusting to my care Your most beloved virgin Mary! I could wish for nothing estimable, for in her my spirit finds everything for which it yearns. Her words provide for me abundant consolation. Mary is a jewel which I shall treasure more and more."[135]

---

[134] Maria Cecilia Baij, *The Life of Saint Joseph* (Asbury, NJ: 101 Foundation, 2000), 76.
[135] Baij, *The Life of Saint Joseph*, 81.

Alexandre-François Caminade. *Le Mariage de la Vierge*. 1824.

St. Joseph of Cupertino

"He sought to show her a love than which none could be more tender and deep... He adorned her images with flowers and devoted the most fervent affections of his heart to her. He was wont to say jestingly: 'My mother is very strange; if I bring her flowers, she says she does not want them; if I bring her cherries, she will not take them, and if I then ask her what she desires, she replies: 'I desire thy heart; for I live on hearts!'"[136]

---

[136] Angelo Pastrovicchi, *St. Joseph of Copertino* (Rockford, IL: TAN, 1980), 51-52.

"Once, when the Litany of Our Lady was being prayed in the church, he flew over six fellow religious at the words 'Hail Mary.' At other times such flights occurred at the words, 'Holy Mother of God,' 'Mother of Divine Grace,' 'Gate of Heaven.' Even on hearing the name of Mary he was often enraptured and lifted from the ground. His heart melted at the thought of the beauty of the Queen of Heaven. One day, while he was saying Mass, many persons saw him enraptured and lifted into the air and heard him exclaim with tears in his eyes, 'Praise her, ye holy angels, with your songs; for I pine away because I cannot worthily praise her.'"[137]

"Not satisfied that Mary should be loved and praised by all the saints and angels of Paradise, he most earnestly desired that she be loved and praised by all men on earth."[138]

"What Office? What rosary? ... My Lady wishes more, she desires the heart and the will."[139]

"The servant of God had acquired such confidence in his heavenly Mother that by reciting the Litany he was able to exorcise devils and free the possessed. In serious dissensions he reconciled the litigants by saying to them, "Let us go to Mother, to Mother.""[140]

"To be brief, Joseph's holiness began, as he himself attested, with devotion to Mary…During his whole life our saint called the Blessed Virgin 'Mother' and in dying he invoked her by that sweet name in the words of the Ave Maris Stella:

> Show thyself a Mother;
> Offer Him our sighs,
> Who for us Incarnate

---

[137] Pastrovicchi, *St. Joseph of Copertino*, 52.
[138] Pastrovicchi, *St. Joseph of Copertino*, 53.
[139] Pastrovicchi, *St. Joseph of Copertino*, 53.
[140] Pastrovicchi, *St. Joseph of Copertino*, 54.

Did not thee despise."[141]

St. Juan Diego

"Mary calls St. Juan Diego eleven times 'Noxocoyouh', 'my fructification' ('Xocóyotl'), a word which in itself does not mean 'son', but it was the title given to the youngest child in the family, who was considered the dearest, most precious one. In other words, it is a term that shows great tenderness and esteem, and is still used in Mexico today ('mi xocoyote', 'mi xocoyotito'). Mary starts every dialogue with St. Juan Diego with this word (Cf. nn.23; 58; 90; 107; 137), and repeats it when she is going to reveal something very important (Cf. nn. 26; 60; 92; 118; 125) (end: n.37). St. Juan Diego himself addresses Mary several times with this same word (cf. n.50;)."[142]

Keith Berubé

"A Consecration Prayer of Offering to Console Mary"

"Mary, my life and my sweetness, I give myself totally to you, I give my heart to you and take your Heart as my own. I want to console you in your sorrows, remove thorns from your Heart, love your Heart as dearer than my own, and in so doing place the balm of requited love upon your Heart.

Jesus, give me this grace: to truly requite Mary's love for me, and to console her in her sorrows. On my own, Jesus, I cannot; but if you and I are one, then I can, because then it is not I that live, but you that live in me and as one with me, and then she can lean upon me. 'Who is this that cometh

---

[141] Pastrovicchi, *St. Joseph of Copertino*, 56.
[142] Deyanira Flores, "The Rich Mariological Doctrine of the Nican Mopohua," at Marian Congress, at www.mariancongress.org, IV. A. 4. "The Titles Used."

up from the desert, flowing with delights, leaning upon her beloved?' (Canticles 8:5).

Not that Mary, the Strong Woman of Proverbs 31, *needs* to lean upon me—I need to lean upon her! ('She will feed him with the bread of understanding, and give him the water of wisdom to drink. He will lean on her and will not fall, and he will rely on her and will not be put to shame,' Sirach 15:3-4). But let me console her, as her beloved, to whom she can look to and rely on for comfort in her sorrow.

So lean on me, my most precious Mary, who loves me with the purest love of every womanly love, with all the loves of mother, sister and spouse, you who were entrusted to me at the Cross by Jesus in his holy Passion as I was entrusted to you. Lean on my prayers, sufferings, mortifications and Holy Communions offered to you in penance for sins and to save souls with you.

Be comforted, my sorrowful Mary, because I love you with all my heart and mind and will, as Jesus loves you. Your love in me is requited! I am all yours, I love you as my Mother, sister and spouse, as you love me with all these loves ('She will come to meet him like a mother, and like the wife of his youth she will welcome him,' Sirach 15:2), and I take you for all mine with praise and thanksgiving to Our Father.

May we and all those souls we save from Hell rejoice with him in his house forever more. Amen."[143]

"...for each member of Christ Mary is 'My Girl,' this is living God's life...this is your life: We are each the Father's son who gets the Princess, we are each the apple of Mary's eye: 'She [Mary] saw her Son in all his members.'

As the saying goes, 'This changes everything!' When the pauper realizes he is really a prince and he's given a kingdom and a princess he changes his

---

[143] Keith Berube, *Mary, the Beloved* (St. Louis, MO: En Route, 2017), 329-330.

ways, if he's wise. This is our choice on earth. If we don't know this, know it in our very bones, we can fall into the trap of thinking that Marian devotion, let's call it love, is optional. But devotion to Mary is loving Mary, and after loving God this is Jesus's life—from eternity the Word totally gives himself to her."[144]

"Mary has known you for over 2000 years. She knew and loved you before your mother, wife, siblings, anyone. She sacrificed her Son and suffered with him the most grievous martyrdom for you. No one loves you like Mary. She is the first relationship you had with a human person, though you didn't know it then, and she is the one we are meant, and who we ought (as a moral obligation), to love most after God, though we often get things backwards: We tend to think that Mary's place in our lives comes after mother, father, wife, children, siblings, friends; rather, Mary has the first place in our lives after and yet also with God. The mother of at least one Saint even saw herself, accurately, as a nursemaid-stand-in for Mary, the true mother of her child!

Why mention this? Because we can be shy in loving Mary, thinking others, especially one's biological mother or spouse, ought to come before Mary, or that we might love Mary too much. These are false notions, as is clear from everything that's been said thus far; and as the well-known saying of St. Maximilian Kolbe goes, you cannot love Mary too much, since you cannot possibly love her more than Jesus does. If one loves God first and then Mary, then everyone else, all of one's relationships will bloom!

Indeed, we must beg God to give us his love for Mary so we can love her as we ought. And while emotions are not an accurate barometer of the spiritual life, we must seek to love Mary with a comprehensive love, with all our heart, will, affections and emotions, too: The love we have for Mary should not be an anemic, old, boring, insipid love, as if one was sitting on

---

[144] Keith Berube, *Mary: The Rosary, the Relationship, and Dragons* (St. Louis, MO: En Route, 2020), 12-13.

the couch in old age sipping prune juice! Whether one is a teenager or an elderly man or woman, single, priest, religious, or married, one's love for Mary ought to be passionate, with all the fire of youthful first love, with all the adamant faithfulness and bonding of a little child for his mom, with all the powers of one's soul and body, loving her vigorously, with love burning, blazing, vehement, zealous. We won't always feel this way, but our love for her is proven when we love her even in exhaustion and feelings of boredom and desolation. *This* is how to love Mary. This is how Jesus loves Mary, this is how the Saints love Mary. It is with this passion— hot, not cold, nor lukewarm—that she loves us. God does not want us to love Mary as if we were absent-mindedly saying, "Sure, that's great" to a used vacuum salesman. Don't be afraid to let yourself fall in love with Mary; it's the best thing you can do for yourself and everyone you care about."[145]

St. Leonard of Port Maurice

"I strongly wish to die in order to live with Mary. Recite a Hail Mary for me. Obtain the grace for me to die now in this pulpit. I want to go see Mary."[146]

Louis Kaczmarek

"When a day comes that we feel tired in this struggle against the powers of darkness, let us immediately remind ourselves that Mary's beautiful eyes are upon us and She is smiling and thanking us for the love and sacrifice we are putting forth. We cannot fail Her or disappoint Her. Her happiness and Her smile mean everything to us.

---

[145] Berube, *Mary: The Rosary, the Relationship, and Dragons*, 112-113.
[146] Manelli, *Devotion to Our Lady*, 37.

We can face the infernal enemy with Our Lady at our side to protect us. We will do all She asks and repeat often, 'Totus Tuus' (I am All Yours)!"[147]

"Let us bravely show to everyone our love for Our Blessed Mother."[148]

St. Louis de Montfort

"Oh, how happy is the man who has given everything to Mary, and has entrusted himself to Mary, and lost himself in her, in everything and for everything! He belongs all to Mary and Mary belongs all to him. He can say boldly with David: 'Mary is made for me' (Cf. *Ps.* 118:56); or with the beloved disciple: 'I have taken her for my own' (*Jn.* 19:27); or with Jesus Christ: 'All that I have is thine, and all that thou hast is Mine.' (*Jn.* 17:10)."[149]

"Indeed you may without hesitation say to her, 'I am yours, O Blessed Virgin, obtain salvation for me,' or with the beloved disciple, St. John, 'I have taken you, Blessed Mother, for my all.' Or again you may say with St. Bonaventure, 'Dear Mother of saving grace, I will do everything with confidence and without fear because you are my strength and my boast in the Lord,' or in another place, 'I am all yours and all that I have is yours, O glorious Virgin, blessed above all created things. Let me place you as a seal upon my heart, for your love is as strong as death.' Or adopting the sentiments of the prophet, 'Lord, my heart has no reason to be exalted nor should my looks be proud; I have not sought things of great moment nor wonders beyond my reach; nevertheless, I am still not humble. But I have roused my soul and taken courage. I am as a child, weaned from earthly pleasures and resting on its mother's breast. It is upon this breast that all good things come to me.'"[150]

---

[147] Kaczmarek, *Mary and the Power of God's Love*, 53.

[148] Kaczmarek, *Mary and the Power of God's Love*, 132.

[149] Louis de Montfort, *True Devotion*, trans. Frederick William Faber (Rockford, IL: TAN, 1985), §179.

[150] Montfort, *True Devotion*, §216.

"Chosen souls, slaves of Jesus in Mary, understand that after the Our Father, the Hail Mary is the most beautiful of all prayers. It is the perfect compliment the most High God paid to Mary through his archangel in order to win her heart. So powerful was the effect of this greeting upon her, on account of its hidden delights, that despite her great humility, she gave her consent to the incarnation of the Word."[151]

"The Hail Mary is a heavenly dew which fertilizes the soul. It is the chaste and loving kiss which we give to Mary. It is a vermilion rose which we present to her; a precious pearl we offer her; a chalice of divine ambrosial nectar which we proffer to her."[152]

M. Henri Lasserre

"The Mother of our Lord Jesus Christ had not said: 'I am Mary immaculate." She had said, 'I am the Immaculate Conception;' as if to mark the absolute character, the substantial character in some sort, of the divine privilege which she alone had had since Adam and Eve were created by God. It is as if she had said, not 'I am pure,' but, 'I am purity itself;' not 'I am a Virgin,' but 'I am Virginity living and Incarnate;' not 'I am spotless,' but 'Spotlessness itself.' A thing that is white may cease to be so, but whiteness is always white; it is its essence, not its quality."[153]

---

[151] Montfort, *True Devotion*, §252.
[152] Montfort, *True Devotion*, §253.
[153] M. Henri Lasserre, *Bernadette* (Derby, England: Richardson and Son: 1879), 152.

Piotr Stachiewicz. *Making Wreaths.* 1894.

Venerable Maria Teresa Quevedo

"Teresa's sufferings [tremendous sufferings in the last stages of tuberculous meningitis; she died a 19-year-old fully professed Carmelite nun] were assuaged by the comfort that came from her love for Our Lady. Alone most of the time, she conversed with her. 'How deeply I suffer,' she would tell her. 'All for you, sweet Lady. All for Jesus through my Mother Mary…. Sweet Lady, I am very sick. I offer you this illness…. I trust in you, Mary, my Mother…. Mary, my Mistress, I obey you…. I love you, Queen of my heart!'"[154]

"'The words she spoke to Our Lady as I sat with her,' wrote Sister Maria Segura, 'are words I shall never forget: 'My dear Mother Mary, I have tried to be perfect for your sake…. Now you will take me with you to Heaven…. My Jesus, I love You for those who do not love You…. My Mother, I would rather die a thousand times than offend you once…. Jesus, I have loved only You and my dear Mother Mary.'"[155]

"Broken words bespoke a complete holocaust to Our Lady: 'I am all yours… O my Mother… for you I was born… for you I die…. What do you wish… my Mother… of me? I am all yours… all yours… all yours…. O Mother of love… cover me… with your… mantle of blue…. How beautiful she is…. How good…she is…'"[156]

[Seeing Mary moments before her death] "Looking up with wide eyes, an angelic smile on her face, she said, 'How beautiful! O Mary, how beautiful you are! [Earlier] Teresita had begged, 'My Mother, come for me,' and the Queen and Love of her life, indulging her child to the end, responded to that call."[157]

---

[154] Mary Pierre, *Mary was Her Life* (New York: Benziger, 1960), 218.
[155] Pierre, *Mary was Her Life,* 221.
[156] Pierre, *Mary was Her Life,* 222.
[157] Pierre, *Mary was Her Life,* 227.

Dom Mark Daniel Kirby

"In your face, O little Mary, we already see that of Jesus; in your voice, we already hear His. Your voice, O little Mary, is sweet to our ears; your face is lovely to our eyes, for He whom the whole universe cannot contain will be enclosed in your womb. He will grow for nine months beneath your Immaculate Heart. Out of your flesh and blood the Holy Spirit will form a human Heart for the Son of God, the very Heart that, together with yours, will be pierced on Calvary.

You, O little Mary, Maria Bambina, are the Cause of our Joy! Your appearance in the arms of your mother announces that the Word of the Father, God from God, Light from Light, True God from True God, will soon appear in your arms. And you have but one desire, one joy: to give us your Son, to draw us to Him, that your joy might be ours and that our joy might be fulfilled."[158]

---

[158] Mark Kirby, "Maria Bambina," *Vultus Christi* (8 September 2008), at vultus.stblogs.org.

Dante Gabriel Rossetti. *The Girlhood of Mary Virgin.* 1849.

St. Maximilian Kolbe

[From a letter relating his well-nigh torturous journey on a ship] "To tell the truth, I suffered greatly ... it seemed to me as if I was failing ... I would have liked to get up and move myself, but then there came a cold sweat and the vomiting of sea-sickness … My headache did not decrease … My only relief was the mental invocation which I made frequently, very frequently, of the Most Holy Name of Mary. Perhaps, in my delirium from the fever, I even forget to do this at certain times. Then I began to feel a little better; I opened my suitcase to see what they had put in it for us. I began to unpack it and…behold, the small head of a little statue of the Immaculate. How could I resist from kissing her with tenderness? … Are we not but one heart in Her?"[159]

"Sweet Heart of Mary, make me love you like crazy!" [A more literal translation however is "Sweet Heart of Mary, make me love you/bring it about that I love you unto foolishness/madness/lunacy," cf. the note from Manelli concerning this in his book.][160]

A Rule of Life for Those Consecrated to the Immaculate Virgin

1. It is my duty to be a saint and a great saint.
2. For the glory of God, I must save myself and all souls, present and future, through the Immaculate.
3. Before anything else flee not only from mortal but also from deliberate venial sin.
4. Do not permit: a. that evil remain without reparation and destruction; or b. that good be without fruit or increase.
5. Let your rule be obedience, the will of God through the Immaculate, I am nothing but an instrument.
6. Think of what you are doing. Do not be concerned about anything else, whether bad or good.
7. Preserve order, and order will preserve you.

---

[159] Stefano Manelli, *The Marian Vow* (New Bedford, MA: Academy of the Immaculate, 2010), 45.
[160] Manelli, *The Marian Vow*, 151.

8. Peaceful and benevolent action.

9. Preparation—Action—Conclusion.

10. Remember that you belong exclusively, unconditionally, absolutely, irrevocably to the Immaculate: Whoever you are, whatever you have or can, whatever you do (thoughts, words, action) and endure (pleasant, unpleasant, indifferent things) belong to the Immaculate. Consequently, may she dispose of them according to Her will (and not yours). In the same way it belongs to Her all your intentions; therefore, may she transform them, add others, take them away, as She likes (in fact, She does not offend justice).

You are an instrument in Her hand, therefore do only what She wants; accept everything like a child to his own mother, trust Her in everything. Take an interest about Her, Her veneration, Her things and let Her take care of you and your loved ones. Recognize that everything you have comes from Her and nothing from you. All the fruits of your activities depend on the union with Her, in the same way as She is an instrument of the divine mercy.

O Immaculate, my life (every moment of it), my death (where, when and how) and my eternity belongs totally to you. Of everything You do whatever You like."[161]

---

[161] Maximillian Kolbe, "A Rule of Life for Those Consecrated to the Immaculate Virgin," at Franciscan Archive, at http://franciscan-archive.org/franciscana/prayers.html.

Antonio Cortina y Farinós. *Immaculate Conception*. 1876.

St. Mechtilde

Jesus to St. Mechtilde in the year 1300:

"I am now addressing those who have a special veneration for the most worthy Heart of my virginal Mother. I myself have rooted in your hearts your ardent desire of honoring Her Heart as I wish it to be honored. I know that, as her Heart is the first object of the love of my Heart, after the Eternal Father, it is likewise, after God, the first object of your most tender and holy affection. Therefore have I given it to you to be an inexhaustible fountain of blessings in your midst. I have given my Mother's Heart to you as a divine Sun to enlighten you through the darkness of the world, to warm you in the frosts of mortal life, to gladden and to comfort you in the sorrows, pains and miseries of earth, and to vivify and strengthen you against the decline and weakness of human frailty. I have given her Heart to you as a beautiful mirror, into which you should often gaze in order to see the stains that tarnish your Souls, so that you may cleanse them. With the aid of this celestial mirror, you should array your Souls with becoming ornaments that they may become pleasing in the sight of my divine majesty.

I have likewise given you the admirable Heart of my most worthy Mother, which is identified with my own Heart, that it may be your true Heart as well; that my children may possess only one Heart with their Mother, and my members the same Heart as their Head. Thus you may serve, adore and love God with a Heart worthy of His infinite goodness: *Corde magno et animo volenti,* (3) that is, with an immense and measureless Heart, with a Heart all pure and holy, so that you may sing His divine praises and accomplish all your actions in the spirit, love, humility and all the holy dispositions of her admirable Heart. But in order to make this come true, you must renounce entirely your own heart, that is, your mind, your will and your love of self. Strive, therefore, to rid yourself of your earthly heart that is depraved and wicked, and you shall receive an entirely heavenly, holy and divine Heart. I have finally given this marvelous Heart as an inestimable treasure containing every possible blessing. It is for you, beloved children, to engrave in your hearts a high esteem, a profound respect and a particular affection for so rich a treasure, and to preserve it jealously by the continuation and increase of your veneration for a Heart so holy and amiable."[162]

---

[162] John Eudes, *The Admirable Heart of Mary* (New York: P.J. Kenedy & Sons, 1948), 107-109.

Pompeo Girolamo Batoni. *Holy Family with Sts Elizabeth and John the Baptist.* 1777.

Fr. Michael Gaitley

"When we experience Mary's tender care for us, we'll fall more in love with her. But we have to speak with her. We have to ask her. And what if, even after many signs of her love and care, we still don't feel love for the Immaculata or her love for us? Kolbe explains:

> Never worry that you don't feel this love. If you have the will to love, you already give a proof that you love. What counts is the will to love. External feeling is also a fruit of grace, but it does not always follow the will. Sometimes, my dear ones, the thought, a sad longing, as if a plea or a complaint, may occur to you: 'Does the Immaculata still love me?' Most beloved children! I tell you all and each one individually, in her name (mark that: in her name!), she loves every one of you. She loves you very much at every moment with no exception. This…I repeat for you in her name."[163]

Modesto P. Sa-onoy (20th century)

"The word 'Rosary' comes from the Latin word, 'rosarium' which means 'rose garden' or 'garland of roses'. The old Middle English used 'rosarie' from which we derive the present spelling. The adoption of the term traced back to the ancient tradition that Our Lady revealed to several people that each time they say a Hail Mary they are giving her a beautiful rose and that each complete Rosary makes her a crown or garland of roses. The beads represent

---

[163] Michael Gaitley, *33 Days to Morning Glory* (Stockbridge, MA: Marian, 2013), 112.

the roses...It can seem a repetitive prayer but instead it is like two sweethearts who many times say to one another the words: 'I love you'..."[164] [The Painting below, while created as an image of the myth "Daphnis and Chloe," upon which Shakespeare's "The Winter's Tale" (an eminently Catholic and Marian play) is in part based, is a beautiful image of the intimate love between Mary and the one who prays the Rosary, of we who are mired in sins and faults while yet on this earth and she who is Immaculate beauty but does not disdain our love. Note the purple--an apt color here, since purple is the color of royalty, kings and queens.]

---

[164] Modesto P. Sa-onoy, "Holy Rosary—A Super Weapon," at The Daily Guardian at https://thedailyguardian.net.

Elizabeth Jane Gardner. *Daphnis and Chloe.* 1882.

St. Padre Pio

"St. Pio of Pietrelcina recounts that one day, having Our Lady at his side, it seemed to him as if She truly '*had nothing else to think about but me alone, filling my heart with holy affections.*'"[165]

"St. Pio of Pietrelcina, as is well-known, was aflame with such a love for the Madonna that he became all fire in his heart. He himself said that he felt '*a mysterious fire coming from his heart,*' a fire of love so ardent as to constrain him to have '*ice applied to him in order to extinguish so intense a fire.*' What, on the other hand, is our heart like?"[166]

Venerable Patrick Peyton

"...in discovering Mary I discovered a protector. I found a friend. I found a mother that would never die. I found a mother filled with affection for me, filled with concern for my welfare, lavishing upon me her strength, her prayers, her guidance, her protection."[167]

Venerable Pauline Jaricot

"Early in the morning of January 9, 1862, Pauline cried out in her last words: 'Mary, my Mother, I am all yours!'"[168]

---

[165] Manelli, *The Marian Vow*, 38.
[166] Manelli, *The Marian Vow*, 96.
[167] Calloway, *Champions of the Rosary*, 301.
[168] Ann Ball, *Modern Saints, Their Lives and Faces: Book Two* (Rockford, IL: TAN, 1990), 80.

William Adolphe Bouguereau. *Virgin and Lamb*. 1903.

St. Philip Neri

"Our Blessed Lady ought to be our love and our consolation."[169]

---

[169] Will Bloomfield, "The Daily Sayings of St. Philip Neri," at Sacred Art Series Blog, at http://sacredartseries.blogspot.com.

Raïssa Maritain

"The Blessed Virgin is the spoiled child of the Blessed Trinity...She knows no law. Everything yields to her in heaven and on earth. The whole of heaven gazes on her with delight. She plays before the ravished eyes of God himself."[170]

Raymond F. Roseliep

"Symphony in Blue"

The gentian sleep in waters
That are a maiden's eyes;
The maiden wears a mantle
Cut from the morning's skies.

A wheel of stars is whirling
About her dawn-veiled hair;
The sparks flash blue and silver
Above the serpent's lair

The maiden tends a fountain
Of Rain for grape and wheat,
Its torrent is immersing
The blue globe at her feet.[171]

---

[170] Mark Kirby, "Maria Bambina," *Vultus Christi* (8 September 2008), at vultus.stblogs.org.
[171] M. Therese, *I Sing of a Maiden*, 360.

Giovanni Battista Trotti. *Mary Architect of the Universe.* 1603.

Charles Amable Lenoir. *A Nymph in the Forest.* n.d.

Richard Crashaw (1613-1649)

Excerpt from "On the Glorious Assumption of Our Blessed Lady"
Thy pretious Name shall be
Thy self to us; and we
With holy care will keep it by us.
We to the last
Will hold it fast
And no Assumption shall deny us.
All the sweetest show'res
Of our fairest flow'res
Will we strow upon it.
Though our sweets cannot make
It sweeter, then can take
Themselves new sweetness from it.
Maria, men and Angels sing
Maria, mother of our King.
Live, rosy princesse, Live. And may the bright
Crown of a most incomprehensible light
Embrace thy radiant browes. O may the best
Of everlasting joys bathe thy white breast.
Live, our chast love, the holy mirth
Of heav'n; the humble pride of earth.
Live, crown of women; Queen of men.
Live mistress of our son. And when
Our weak desires have done their best,
Sweet Angels come, and sing the rest.[172]

---

[172] M. Therese, *I Sing of a Maiden*, 142.

Robert Menth (20th century)

"Cry from the Battlefield"

O Lady, together with the Child you take
In your frail arms to hush His frightened cries,
Cradle us against your heart and ache
To see the sorrow starting from our eyes.
O Lady strong beyond all ecstasy,
Young willow bent before the breath of God,
Think still of us as little ones while we
Thrust puny chests at Heaven from this sod
And flail with futile fits against the Breast
Where beats the Beauty passion cannot taste.
O Lady, heal our wars, our dark unrest,
The lusts that lash our land a scarlet waste:
Mother of men, this bleeding face
Awaits the wonder of your love's embrace.[173]

Monsignor Ronald Knox

"I think she is, in a sense, closer to us nowadays than she was to earlier generations of Christians. She is something more to us than a theological symbol; nor do we think of her, in the manner of the Middle Ages, as the patroness of this or that institution, a religious order, or a parish, or a guild. Rather, to each of us, she is a personal romance."[174]

---

[173] M. Therese, *I Sing of a Maiden*, 365.
[174] Ronald Knox, "The Priestly Life," *EWTN* (1958), at http://ewtn.com, chapter 13.

Roy Schoeman

"I was left alone with the most beautiful young woman I could ever imagine, and I knew without being told that it was the most Blessed Virgin Mary…when I woke up I was hopelessly in love with the Blessed Virgin Mary."[175]

"I went to sleep and I thought I was awoken by a gentle hand on my shoulder and led to a room and left alone with the most beautiful young woman I could ever imagine. I knew without being told that it was the Blessed Virgin Mary. When I found myself in her presence, all I wanted to do was fall on my knees and worship her appropriately. In fact the only thought that crossed my mind was, 'Oh my God, I wish I at least knew the Hail Mary, to honor her,' but I didn't.

I was just overwhelmed — overwhelmed — just lifted into ecstasy by her love, and as beautiful as she was to look at, more affective was the sound of her voice. When she spoke, her voice was like what makes music music — the essence of music — and with it was a love that just flowed through all of my fibers and lifted me up into an ecstasy."[176]

Fr. Stefano Manelli

"Our Lady is God's masterpiece of love, of every love God has instilled in creatures—motherly love, filial love, spousal love, virginal love."[177]

---

[175] Roy Schoeman, "Jewish Harvard Professor Roy Schoeman Becomes Convinced Catholic (Talk 1 Prescott Mission)," at YouTube, at www.youtube.com.

[176] Roy Schoeman, "Virgin Mary appears to Harvard Professor Part 1 (Jewish Convert to Catholic)," at YouTube, at www.youtube.com.

[177] Manelli, *Devotion to Our Lady*, 35.

St. Teresa of Avila

"I want to be after Our Lord the one who has loved Mary the most."[178]

St. Therese

"The Blessed Virgin is the Queen of heaven and earth, quite true, but she is more mother than queen...It is proper to speak of her prerogatives, but we must not content ourselves with that. We must do all we can to make her beloved of souls."[179]

[Asked in her sickness if Mary was hiding from her]: "No, the Blessed Virgin will never be hidden from me, for I love her too much."[180]

[Her last written words, on the back of a picture of Our Lady of Victories]: "O Mary, if I were Queen of heaven and you were Therese, I would rather become Therese, that you might be the Queen of heaven."[181]

---

[178] Manelli, *Devotion to Our Lady*, 28.

[179] Francoise Jamart, *Complete Spiritual Doctrine of St. Therese of Lisieux* (Staten Island, NY: Alba House, 1961), 255.

[180] Jamart, *Complete Spiritual Doctrine of St. Therese of Lisieux*, 259.

[181] Jamart, *Complete Spiritual Doctrine of St. Therese of Lisieux*, 260.

Elizabeth Jane Gardner. *The Improvised Cup.* Circa 1884.

Giovanni Battista Salvi da Sassoferrato. *Virgin Mary at Prayer.* 1640-1650.

Why I Love You, O Mary!

Oh! I would like to sing, Mary, why I love you,
  Why your sweet name thrills my heart,

111

And why the thought of your supreme greatness
Could not bring fear to my soul.
If I gazed on you in your sublime glory,
Surpassing the splendor of all the blessed,
I could not believe that I am your child.
O Mary, before you I would lower my eyes!…

If a child is to cherish his mother,
She has to cry with him and share his sorrows.
O my dearest Mother, on this foreign shore
How many tears you shed to draw me to you!…
In pondering your life in the holy Gospels,
I dare look at you and come near you.
It's not difficult for me to believe I'm your child,
For I see you human and suffering like me…

When an angel from Heaven bids you be the Mother
O the God who is to reign for all eternity,
I see you prefer, O Mary, what a mystery!
The ineffable treasure of virginity.
O Immaculate Virgin, I understand how your soul
Is dearer to the Lord than his heavenly dwelling.
I understand how your soul, Humble and Sweet Valley,
Can contain Jesus, the Ocean of Love!…

Oh! I love you, Mary, saying you are the servant
Of the God whom you charm by your humility.
This hidden virtue makes you all-powerful.
It attracts the Holy Trinity into your heart.
Then the Spirit of Love covering you with his shadow,
The Son equal to the Father became incarnate in you,

There will be a great many of his sinner brothers,
Since he will be called : Jesus, your first-born!…

O beloved Mother, despite my littleness,
Like you I possess The All-Powerful within me.
But I don't tremble in seeing my weakness;
The treasures of a mother belong to her child,
And I am your child, O my dearest Mother.
Aren't your virtues and your love mine too?
So when the white Host comes into my heart,
Jesus, your Sweet Lamb, thinks he is resting in you!…

You make me feel that it's not impossible
To follow in your footsteps, O Queen of the elect.
You made visible the narrow road to Heaven
While always practicing the humblest virtues.
Near you, Mary, I like to stay little.
I see the vanity of greatness here below.
At the home of Saint Elizabeth, receiving your visit,
I learn how to practice ardent charity.

There, Sweet Queen of angels, I listen, delighted,
To the sacred canticle springing forth from your heart.
You teach me to sing divine praises,
To glory in Jesus my Savior.
Your words of love are mystical roses
Destined to perfume the centuries to come.
In you the Almighty has done great things.
I want to ponder them to bless him for them.

When good Saint Joseph did not know of the miracle
That you wanted to hide in your humility,
You let him cry close by the Tabernacle
Veiling the Savior's divine beauty!…
Oh Mary! how I love your eloquent silence!
For me it is a sweet, melodious concert
That speaks to me of the greatness and power
Of a soul which looks only to Heaven for help…

Later in Bethlehem, O Joseph and Mary!
I see you rejected by all the villagers.
No one wants to take in poor foreigners.
There's room for the great ones…
There's room for the great ones, and it's in a stable
That the Queen of Heaven must give birth to a God.
O my dearest Mother, how lovable I find you,
How great I find you in such a poor place!…

When I see the Eternal God wrapped in swaddling clothes,
When I hear the poor cry of the Divine Word,
O my dearest Mother, I no longer envy the angels,
For their Powerful Lord is my dearest Brother!…
How I love you, Mary, you who made
This Divine Flower blossom on our shores!…
How I love you listening to the shepherds and wisemen
And keeping it all in your heart with care!…

I love you mingling with the other women
Walking toward the holy temple.
I love you presenting the Savior of our souls
To the blessed Old Man who pressed Him to his heart.

At first I smile as I listen to his canticle,
But soon his tone makes me shed tears.
Plunging a prophetic glance into the future,
Simeon presents you with a sword of sorrows.

O Queen of martyrs, till the evening of your life
That sorrowful sword will pierce your heart.
Already you must leave your native land
To flee a king's jealous fury.
Jesus sleeps in peace under the folds of your veil.
Joseph comes begging you to leave at once,
And at once your obedience is revealed.
You leave without delay or reasoning.

O Mary, it seems to me that in the land of Egypt
Your heart remains joyful in poverty,
For is not Jesus the fairest Homeland,
What does exile matter to you? You hold Heaven…
But in Jerusalem a bitter sadness
Comes to flood your heart like a vast ocean.
For three days, Jesus hides from your tenderness.
That is indeed exile in all its harshness!…

At last you find him and you are overcome with joy,
You say to the fair Child captivating the doctors:
"O my Son, why have you done this?
Your father and I have been searching for you in tears."
And the Child God replies (O what a deep mystery!)
To his dearest Mother holding out her arms to him:
"Why were you searching for me?
I must be about My Father's business. Didn't you know?"

The Gospel tells me that, growing in wisdom,
Jesus remains subject to Joseph and Mary,
And my heart reveals to me with what tenderness
He always obeys his dear parents.
Now I understand the mystery of the temple,
The hidden words of my Lovable King.
Mother, your sweet Child wants you to be the example
Of the soul searching for Him in the night of faith.

Since the King of Heaven wanted his Mother
To be plunged into the night, in anguish of heart,
Mary, is it thus a blessing to suffer on earth?
Yes, to suffer while loving is the purest happiness!…
All that He has given me, Jesus can take back.
Tell him not to bother with me…
He can indeed hide from me, I'm willing to wait for him
Till the day without sunset when my faith will fade away…

Mother full of grace, I know that in Nazareth
You live in poverty, wanting nothing more.
No rapture, miracle, or ecstasy
Embellish your life, O Queen of the Elect!…
The number of little ones on earth is truly great.
They can raise their eyes to you without trembling.
It's by the ordinary way, incomparable Mother,
That you like to walk to guide them to Heaven.

Claudio Coello. *The Holy Family.* Second half of 17th century.

While waiting for Heaven, O my dear Mother,
I want to live with you, to follow you each day.
Mother, contemplating you, I joyfully immerse myself,
Discovering in your heart abysses of love.
Your motherly gaze banishes all my fears.
It teaches me to cry, it teaches me to rejoice.
Instead of scorning pure and simple joys,
You want to share in them, you deign to bless them.

At Cana, seeing the married couple's anxiety
Which they cannot hide, for they have run out of wine,
In your concern you tell the Savior,
Hoping for the help of his divine power.
Jesus seems at first to reject your prayer:
"Woman, what does this matter," he answers, "to you and to me?"
But in the depths of his heart, He calls you his Mother,
And he works his first miracle for you…

One day when sinners are listening to the doctrine
Of Him who would like to welcome them in Heaven,
Mary, I find you with them on the hill.
Someone says to Jesus that you wish to see him.
Then, before the whole multitude, your Divine Son
Shows us the immensity of his love for us.
He says: "Who is my brother and my sister and my Mother,
If not the one who does my will?"

O Immaculate Virgin, most tender of Mothers,
In listening to Jesus, you are not saddened.
But you rejoice that He makes us understand
How our souls become his family here below.

Yes, you rejoice that He gives us his life,
The infinite treasures of his divinity!...
How can we not love you, O my dear Mother,
On seeing so much love and so much humility?

You love us, Mary, as Jesus loves us,
And for us you accept being separated from Him.
To love is to give everything. It's to give oneself.
You wanted to prove this by remaining our support.
The Savior knew your immense tenderness.
He knew the secrets of your maternal heart.
Refuge of sinners, He leaves us to you
When He leaves the Cross to wait for us in Heaven.

Mary, at the top of Calvary standing beside the Cross
To me you seem like a priest at the altar,
Offering your beloved Jesus, the sweet Emmanuel,
To appease the Father's justice...
A prophet said, O afflicted Mother,
"There is no sorrow like your sorrow!" O Queen of Martyrs, while
remaining in exile
You lavish on us all the blood of your heart!

Saint John's home becomes your only refuge.
Zebedee's son is to replace Jesus...
That is the last detail the Gospel gives.
It tells me nothing more of the Queen of Heaven.
But, O my dear Mother, doesn't its profound silence
Reveal that The Eternal Word Himself
Wants to sing the secrets of your life
To charm your children, all the Elect of Heaven?

Soon I'll hear that sweet harmony.

Soon I'll go to beautiful Heaven to see you.

You who came to smile at me in the morning of my life,

Come smile at me again … Mother… It's evening now!…

I no longer fear the splendor of your supreme glory.

With you I've suffered and now I want

To sing on your lap, Mary, why I love you,

And to go on saying that I am your child!…[182]

Thomas Kempis

III. Prayer:

Come then, O Mary, sweet Virgin whom I love!

Come then, my hope and my consolation!

Come, for when I am near you, when I hear your voice,

    it seems that I already possess all good,

    it seems that I am sheltered from all evil,

Recalling your sweet clemency,

    I come to seek refuge under your aegis,

    O Mary, you who know how to give

    to the weak, strength,

    to the captive freedom,

    be for me merciful,

    be by your love a mother to me.

Thus I shall know through having experienced it

    how you console with charm,

    and how you defend with assurance,

---

[182] Therese Martin, "Why I love You O Mary!", in *The Poetry of Saint Thérèse of Lisieux,* trans. Donald Kinney (Washington, DC: ICS, 1996), 215-220.

all those who are faithful in serving you.[183]

St. Vincent Pallotti

"I am unworthy of loving our Lady, but by the mercy of God and the merits of Jesus Christ, I desire to obtain the grace of loving her, and it is my wish to love her with the very love which God has for her."[184]

"When he became a priest, he sought to attain a love for the Immaculate mother similar to that which the very persons in the Holy Trinity bore towards her… Pallotti always wanted to honour, love and glorify Mary, even competing with God with a holy envy to love her more: 'I intend, my God, from all eternity and through all eternity, at every infinitesimal moment, to love and to have loved, honored and glorified my most beloved Mother Mary, with the same love, honor and glory which you, O Eternal Father ... You, O Divine Son ... You, Holy Spirit have shown and allowed her (as daughter, mother and most pure bride).'"[185]

"Pallotti always wanted to honour, love and glorify Mary, even competing with God with a holy envy to love her more."[186]

William Shakespeare

[While William Shakespeare did not write directly about Mary, he did fashion characters based on her, and in this way he tells of his deep love for her. Portia, from the *Merchant of Venice*, is perhaps his most obviously Marian character—Portia (her name means "gate") lives far above Venice

---

[183] Thomas a Kempis, *The Imitation of Mary* (Westminster, MD: Newman, 1961), 28.

[184] John Gaynor, *The Life of St. Vincent Pallotti* (Boston, MA: St. Paul Editions, 1980), 61.

[185] Mathew Kanjiramkalayil, "The Role of Mary in the Holiness of St. Vincent Pallotti," at Pallotti Institute, at www.pallottiinstitute.com, 53.

[186] Kanjiramkalayil, "The Role of Mary," 53.

(the world) upon Belmonte (means beautiful mountain and represents Heaven)—Portia is the queen and gate of Belmonte.]

The Merchant of Venice
Act I, Scene I

BASSANIO [Describing Portia to Antonio] In Belmont is a lady richly left,
And she is fair and, fairer than that word,
Of wondrous virtues. Sometimes from her
      eyes
I did receive fair speechless messages.
Her name is Portia—nothing undervalu'd
To Cato's daughter, Brutus' Portia.
Nor is the wide world ignorant of her worth;
For the four winds blow in from every coast
Renowned suiters, and her sunny locks
Hang on her temples like a golden fleece
Which makes her seat of Belmont Colchos'
      strond,
And many Jasons come in quest of her.
O my Antonio, had I but means
To hold a rival place with one of them.
I have a mind presages me such thrift
That I should questionless be fortunate.[187]

---

[187] William Shakespeare, *Merchant of Venice*, Act I, scene i, lines 160-176.

Act III, Scene II

BASSANIO [Finding a portrait of Portia] Fair Portia's counterfeit! What
    demi-god
Hath come so near creation? Move these eyes?
Or whether riding on the balls of mine
Seem they in motion? Here are sever'd lips,
Parted with sugar breath; so sweet a bar
Should sunder such sweet friends. Here in her
    hairs
The painter plays the spider, and hath woven
A golden mesh t' entrap the hearts of men
Faster than gnats in cobwebs. But her eyes—
How could he see to do them? Having made
    one,
Methinks it should have power to steal both his,
And leave itself unfurnish'd. Yet look how far
The substance of my praise doth wrong his
    shadow
In underprizing it, so far this shadow
Doth limp behind the substance.[188]

Act III, Scene II

BASSANIO [to Portia] Madame, you have bereft me of all
    words;
Only my blood speaks to you in my veins;
And there is such confusion in my powers
As, after some oration fairly spoke

---

[188] Shakespeare, *Merchant of Venice*, Act III, scene ii, lines 115-129.

By a beloved prince, there doth appear
Among the buzzing pleased multitude,
Where every something, being blent together,
Turns to a wild of nothing, save of joy
Express'd and not express'd.[189]

Act III, Scene V

LORENZO [to Jessica, about Portia] How dost thou like the Lord
      Bassanio's wife?
JESSICA Past all expressing. It is very meet
The Lord Bassanio live an upright life,
For, having such a blessing in his lady,
He finds the joys of heaven here on earth;
And if on earth he do not merit it,
In reason he should never come to heaven.
Why, if two gods should play some heavenly
      match,
And on the wager lay two earthly women,
And Portia one, there must be something else
Pawn'd with the other; for the poor rude world
Hath not her fellow.[190]

Xavier Perrin

"There is nothing as beautiful as the Blessed Virgin's smile. How could one who was 'full of grace' not be radiant with beauty? If we are not all

---

[189] Shakespeare, *Merchant of Venice*, Act III, scene ii, lines 176-184.
[190] Shakespeare, *Merchant of Venice*, Act III, scene v, lines 63-73.

called, like Saint Catherine Labouré or St. Bernadette, to see the Blessed Virgin with our bodily eyes, we all long to have her beauty revealed to us.

The longing to gaze upon the Immaculate Virgin is not a matter of superficial devotion, of being greedy for sensible consolations, but rather a genuine requirement of Christian contemplation."[191]

---

[191] Xavier Perrin, *The Radiance of Her Face* (Kettering, Ohio: Second Spring, 2017), 5.

Section 2

Mary's Love Letter to us

"The Blessed Virgin, mother of gentleness and mercy, never allows herself to be surpassed in love and generosity. When she sees someone giving himself entirely to her in order to honour and serve her, and depriving himself of what he prizes most in order to adorn her, she gives herself completely in a wondrous manner to him. She engulfs him in the ocean of her graces, adorns him with her merits, supports him with her power, enlightens him with her light, and fills him with her love. She shares her virtues with him—her humility, faith, purity, etc. She makes up for his failings and becomes his representative with Jesus. Just as one who is consecrated belongs entirely to Mary, so Mary belongs entirely to him. We can truthfully say of this perfect servant and child of Mary what St. John in his gospel says of himself, 'He took her for his own.'"[192]

---

[192] Montfort, *True Devotion*, §144.

I

In Scripture

Receive the words of thy handmaid, for if thou wilt follow the words of thy handmaid, the Lord will do with thee a perfect thing.[193]

I love them that love me: and they that in the morning early watch for me, shall find me. With me are riches and glory, glorious riches and justice. For my fruit is better than gold and the precious stone, and my blossoms than choice silver.[194]

…my delights were to be with the children of men. Now therefore, ye children, hear me: Blessed are they that keep my ways. Hear instruction and be wise, and refuse it not. Blessed is the man that heareth me, and that watcheth daily at my gates, and waiteth at the posts of my doors. He that shall find me, shall find life, and shall have salvation from the Lord: But he that shall sin against me, shall hurt his own soul. All that hate me love death.[195]

Whosoever is a little one, let him come to me…Come, eat my bread, and drink the wine which I have mingled for you.[196] For by me shall thy days be multiplied, and years of life shall be added to thee.[197] …he that shall hear me, shall rest without terror, and shall enjoy abundance, without fear of evils.[198]

---

[193] Judith 11:4 *DR*.

[194] Proverbs 8:17-19 *DR*.

[195] Proverbs 8:31-36 *DR*.

[196] Proverbs 9:4-5 *DR* [The Church understands this to be a reference to the Eucharist, the fruit of Mary].

[197] Proverbs 9:11 *DR*.

[198] Proverbs 1:33 *DR*.

Come over to me, all ye that desire me, and be filled with my fruits. For my spirit is sweet above honey, and my inheritance above honey and the honeycomb. My memory is unto everlasting generations.[199]

I will rise, and will go about the city: in the streets and the broad ways I will seek him whom my soul loveth: I sought him, and I found him not. The watchmen who keep the city, found me: Have you seen him, whom my soul loveth?[200] ...they struck me: and wounded me: the keepers of the walls took away my veil from me.[201] When I had a little passed by them, I found him whom my soul loveth: I held him and I will not let him go.[202]

I opened the bolt of my door to my beloved...My soul melted when he spoke.[203]

My beloved to me, and I to him who feedeth among the lilies.[204] Let him kiss me with the kiss of his mouth.[205]

Put me as a seal upon thy heart, as a seal upon thy arm, for love is strong as death.[206]

---

[199] Sirach 24:26-28 *DR.*
[200] Song of Songs 3:2-3 *DR.*
[201] Song of Songs 5:7 *DR.*
[202] Song of Songs 3:4 *DR.*
[203] Song of Songs 5:6 *DR.*
[204] Song of Songs 2:16 *DR.*
[205] Song of Songs 1:1 *DR.*
[206] Song of Songs 8:6 *DR.*

II

Marian Apparitions, Public and Private

Our Lady of Guadalupe, December, 1531

"I am your Merciful Mother and the Mother of all nations on this Earth. I am the Mother of all those who love me, cry to me, and who will place their confidence in me. I will hear their laments, remedy and cure their miseries, misfortunes and sorrows."[207]

"Listen and let it penetrate your heart, my dear little son. Do not be troubled or weighed down with grief. Do not fear any illness or vexation, anxiety or pain. Am I not here who am your Mother? Are you not under my shadow and protection? Am I not your fountain of life? Are you not in the folds of my mantle? In the crossing of my arms? Is there anything else you need?"[208]

[Not content to leave us words only, she left us a portrait of herself for our consolation, so we can see her, as a sweetheart not wanting to leave her lover bereft entirely while he is exiled for a while to the battlefield in a great war...]

---

[207] C. Lourdes Walsh, *The Story of Our Lady of Guadalupe* (Tampa, FL: Mirandapro, 2005), 10.

[208] Francis Johnston, *The Wonder of Guadalupe: The Origin and Cult of the Miraculous Image of the Blessed Virgin in Mexico* (Rockford, IL: TAN, 1981), 33.

Manuel Ramos. *Official Photo of Tilma.* 1923.

Pellevoisin, 1876

[Mary to Estelle Faguette, a woman who saw her fifteen times]: "I am merciful and Mistress of My Son. The few good works and the intense prayers, which you offered me, have touched My Mother-heart, especially that letter which you wrote to me in September. What touched me most was the sentence: 'See the misery of my parents, if I am no longer here, they will soon have to beg for their food. Remember what You suffered when Your Son Jesus Christ was nailed to the cross'. I showed this letter to My Son."[209]

Fatima, Portugal, 1917

"Jesus wants to use you to make me known and loved. He wants to establish in the world the Devotion to my Immaculate Heart. To those who embrace it, I promise salvation. These souls will be loved by God like flowers placed by me to adorn His throne...I will never abandon you. My Immaculate Heart will be your refuge and the way that will lead you God."[210]

Ngome, South Africa, 1955-1971

[10 apparitions; while not yet approving the apparitions, the local bishop, Bishop Mansuet Biyase of the Diocese of Eshowe, has approved the messages, dissemination of the messages, has blessed the altar of the shrine (1992), and allowed open pilgrimages to the shrine, three of which he participated in (1993). In 1999, the diocesan pilgrimage for the Diocese of Eshowe was held at the shrine and attended by Bishop Biyase].

Fourth apparition: March, 15 1956

After Holy Mass, Mary stood before me (serious). She said the following: "My child, I know about your anxiety."

[209] "Mother of Mercy (Pellevoisin, France)," at *365 Days with Mary*, at www.mariancalendar.org.
[210] Joseph Pelletier, *The Sun Danced at Fatima*, (Garden City, NY: Image, 1983), 48.

(She bent down and drew me to herself).

"You asked for a sign?"

Not for me, for the others, that they may believe. They do not believe me.

"I wish that a Shrine be erected for Me in the place where seven springs come together. There I'll let My Graces flow in abundance. Many people shall turn to God."

Sixth apparition: March, 15 1957

"I come to strengthen you. I make use of your nothingness. Be totally humble".

Pausing, She drew me to Herself and said:

"I want to save the world through the Host, My Fruit. I am completely One with the Host as I was One with Jesus under the Cross... Fearful things are in store for you unless you convert."

I asked: *"We?"*

"Yes, if the religious do not convert and if the world does not convert."

Eighth apparition: April, 17 1958

Like a command, Mary said:

"Go to your place. Hurry up, the hour is advanced. I must keep back the streams of Grace with force because you do not make any effort to help Me. I am asking for help from you, My chosen ones."

What are we supposed to do?

"Be hosts. Prepare hosts for Me. Hosts who put themselves completely at My disposal. Only a flaming sea of hosts can drive back the hate of the godless world and retrain the angry Hand of the Father. Don't get tired. I find consolation in revealing Myself to you. I shall never abandon you."

Ninth apparition: March 23, 1970

It was the second night after a horrible appearance of the devil. I was woken from my sleep. All around me was light. Mary Tabernacle of the Most High stood beside me. She took Me into Her Arms and consoled me. She said:

"I know about your anxiety. I stand by you. I shall not abandon you."[211]

Cuapa, Nicaragua, 1980

"Do not be grieved. I am with all of you even though you do not see me. I am the Mother of all of you, sinners. Love one another. Forgive each other. Make peace, because if you don't make it there will be no peace. Do not turn to violence. Never turn to violence. Nicaragua has suffered a great deal since the earthquake and will continue to suffer if all of you don't change. If you don't change you will hasten the coming of the Third World War. Pray, pray, my son, for all the world. A mother never forgets her children. And I have not forgotten what you suffer. I am the Mother of all of you, sinners."[212]

To Blessed Alain de la Roche

"One day, in a Dominican church in Paris, during the All Saints' Day octave, Blessed Alain de la Roche reproached himself for the lukewarm way he was reciting his rosary. Suddenly, Our Lady, accompanied by other virgins appeared before him and said, 'Do not flee, my son! If you don't believe who my companions and I are, just make the sign of the cross before us. If we are hellish visions, we will disappear immediately. If, on the

---

[211] "The Message," at *Ngome Marian Shrine,* at https://ngome.wordpress.com/.

[212] "The Messages of Cuapa," at *The Miracle Hunter,* at http://www.miraclehunter.com/.

contrary, we are heavenly visions, we will remain, and the light that emanates from each one of us will brighten.'

Alain made the sign of the cross and the light of the apparition grew brighter. 'O my son, doubt no more! I am your virginal bride,' Our Lady told him. 'I have always loved you and I am concerned about you always. But you must know that nobody is without pain in this world; neither me, nor my Son, nor any of these saints have lived without suffering. What is more, you must keep the faith and patience as your weapons and prepare yourself for trials more difficult than those which you have experienced up to now. I have chosen you to fight like a brave man and a hero under the flag of Jesus Christ, not like a parody of a soldier! You will stand next to me under my banner. As for the moments of spiritual desert that you have experienced these past few days, don't let them worry you anymore. I wanted you to take that test. Accept it now as a penance and punishment for your past sins. Accept it also as a means of making progress in patience and for the salvations of others, both dead and alive.'

This is how Blessed Alain de la Roche described the apparition that sent him out into the world to preach: Her beauty seemed to reach the summits of what is possible; and, before such beauty, the beauty of flowers, even the beauty of the stars are only a pale copy, a formless shadow, a coarse outline. There exuded from the depths of her physical presence a sweet, powerful and intoxicating perfume. The accent of her voice and her words were so charming-nothing in this world can come close to comparing to her beauty."[213]

To St. Alphonsus Rodriguez

"The blessed Alphonsus Rodriguez, of the Society of Jesus, once prostrate before an image of Mary, felt his heart inflamed with love towards

---

[213] Rene Laurentin, *Dictionnaire des Apparitions* (Paris: Fayard, 2006), 63.

this most Holy Virgin, and burst forth into the following exclamation: 'My most beloved Mother, I know that thou lovest me, but thou dost not love me as much as I love thee.' Mary, as it were, offended and piqued on the point of love, immediately replied from the image: 'What dost thou say, Alphonsus—what dost thou say? O, how much greater is the love that I bear thee, than any love thou canst have for me! Know that the distance between heaven and earth is not so great as the distance between thy love and mine.'"[214]

To St. Bridget of Sweden

"Once Mary told Bridget: 'I am the joy of the just, and the gate to God for sinners. In the fire of Purgatory there is no suffering that through my intercession would not be more easily bearable than otherwise. No one is so damned that, as long as he lives, he will lack my mercy. No one is so far from God, if he is not completely accursed, that he may not come back to God and obtain mercy when he appeals to me.'"

"The Sorrowful Mother of the Crucified Saviour also explained to Bridget that her Immaculate Heart was so full of compassion for the sufferings of sinning humans because she had herself suffered so much from their sins: 'From my Son's birth until His death, I was filled with grief. Tears used to come into my eyes when I gazed at His hands and feet, which the nails were going to pierce…when I meditated on His future Passion…and when I saw the Prophets' saying concerning Him all being fulfilled…And now I look at all the human beings on earth to see whether maybe there are a few who feel compassion for me and who think of my sorrows, but I find very few who meditate on my sufferings and sorrows. Therefore, my daughter, do not forget me, for I am forgotten and ignored by many. See my grief, and imitate me as well as you can. Meditate on my sorrows and my

---

[214] Liguori, *The Glories of Mary*, 40-41.

tears, and mourn that the friends of God are so few…I am grieved over the enemies of my Son in the world who now crucify Him worse than the Jews formerly did. With their vice they crucify my Son in a spiritual way more cruelly and more fearfully than those who crucified Him physically.'"[215]

Émile Munier. *Pardon Mama*. 1888.

"You may ask why your illness has lasted so very long…I answer you— that my Son and I love you…For it is the will of God that the love of men

---

[215] Raphael Brown, *Saints Who Saw Mary* (Charlotte, NC: TAN, 2012), 66.

should correspond to the love of God, and that earlier negligences should be expiated in patience and sickness."[216]

Guardian Angel to St. Gemma Galgani Concerning Mary's Love for Each Person

"Are you fond of Jesus' Mother? Salute Her very often, for She values such attention very much, and unfailingly returns the salutations offered to Her; and if you do not sense this, know that She makes a proof of your unfailing trust."[217]

Mary to St. Gemma Galgani

"Long for me, I too am sighing for you."[218]

To Sister Lucia

[In 1925, Mary appeared with little Jesus to Sr. Lucia; Mary showed Sr. Lucia her Immaculate Heart wrapped with thorns.]
"…and the infant Jesus said, indicating it [Mary's Heart] with His hands: 'Have pity on this loving Heart, a continual martyr to the ingratitude of men.' The Blessed Virgin added: 'See, my child, this Heart of mine, surrounded with thorns with which men transfix it at every moment by their blasphemy and ingratitude. Do you at least try to console me…'"[219]

---

[216] Brown, *Saints Who Saw Mary*, 67.
[217] "St Gemma and Her Guardian Angel," at *St Gemma Galgani* at http://www.stgemmagalgani.com.
[218] Benedict Williamson, *Gemma of Lucca* (St. Louis: Alexander-Ouseley Ltd and B. Herder, 1932), 189.
[219] V. Montes De Oca, *More About Fatima* (Manchester, UK: C. Nicholls, Philips Park, 1971), 91.

Mary to St. John of God

"At the hour of his death Our Lady said these consoling words to St. John of God for the benefit of all devout souls: 'This is the hour in which I am accustomed never to be absent from my devoted servants.'"[220]

Mary to St. Lawrence Justinian

"Approach unto me, all you who desire my love, and I will not reject you, I will not despise you, but will heap upon you those goods with which I abound through my greatness and my noble generation, which made me to be the Mother, Daughter, and Spouse of God. And happy is the soul that yields himself to such sweet invitations, and, from an ungrateful enemy, becomes a faithful friend; from a stranger, becomes a servant; and from an unfaithful one, becomes a most dear and faithful spouse."[221]

To St. Padre Pio

"Another time, when he was all agitated and disturbed, he had a vision of the divine Mother with the Infant Jesus in Her arm; They said to him, *'Calm down! We are with you, you belong to Us and We to you.'* Another helpful episode is this: a confrere asked if Our Lady had ever appeared to him in his cell and Padre Pio immediately responded, *'Rather, ask me if Our Lady has ever left my cell!'*"[222]

---

[220] Manelli, *Devotion to Our Lady*, 39.
[221] Roberto, *The Love of Mary*, 17.
[222] Manelli, *The Marian Vow*, 42.

III

Some Short Commentaries on Mary's Love for Each Person

Fr. Bertrand de Margerie

"But Mary, says Suarez, knows in her Son, seen face to face, all our miseries; she has merited the grace of knowing them and of considering them in her powerful intercession. She begs Christ for us, who are the secondary objects of her beatific vision. Praying for the salvation of her earthly sons, Mary does not consider only the perils affecting them, but also all the particular needs of each one of us."[223]

Fr. Cornelius Hagerty and Venerable Patrick Peyton

"'Our Lady will be as good as you think she is,' he [Fr. Hagerty] said. 'If you think she is a fifty per-center, that is what she will be; if you think she is a hundred per-center, she will be for you a hundred per-center... Even Our Lord and Our Lady do not do as much as they could do,' he added, 'but the reason is that we think they are not able. We limit them by the extent of our faith.'... He went on talking for a long time in this vein, restoring my confidence in the goodness and mercy of God, insisting that the way to reach God was through the intercession of Mary. As I listened, I felt he was building a chasm that spelt the difference between theory and reality, that

---

[223] Bertrand de Margerie, "The Knowledge of Mary and the Sacrifice of Jesus," in *Mary at the Foot of the Cross, Acts of the International Symposium on Marian Coredemption* (New Bedford, MA: Academy of the Immaculate, 2001), 39.

he was leading me across that bridge so that I could see Mary, could walk with her, talk to her, realize that she was a real person who would listen, love, respond. I will not say that I really saw Mary for the first time while he talked, but I know I saw her with a new clarity and intensity, so that I could say in my heart: 'Mother I believe that you are alive, that you are real, that you are a woman, that you have eyes, a face, a smile, a memory, an intelligence, a heart. You have a mother and father of your own. You have a son, who is truly God, who loves you, who will deny you nothing you ask.'

Many beautiful things Father Hagerty said. But what really captivated me was the way he summed up his entire thinking in three brief statements. 'Mary is omnipotent in the power of her prayer,' he said. 'Mary is omnipotent in the power of her intercession with her Son. Mary can do anything God can do.' Then he went on to explain the meaning of these three statements. 'The difference is not in what God can do and what Mary can do. The difference is in the way they do it. God wills something and it happens. Mary prays to Him for something and He does it. He will never say no to her.'

The total impact of what Father Hagerty said was to add a new dimension to the love I already had for the Mother of God. To a greater extent than ever before, he helped me to realize how human she is, how approachable, how sensitive to our needs, so that she could never be haughty or turn her back when we call her."[224]

D. Roberto

"She visits, caresses, and wipes the sweat from the brows of Cistercian monks, wearied with working in the field (*Spec. exempl. ver. Laborare, ex. yo*). She visits and consoles in like manner a dying priest, who had wept over her sorrows (*Cantipr . lib. Ap. apud Sin. cons. 9*). She appears to a young

---

[224] Patrick Peyton, *All for Her* (Hollywood, CA: Family Theater, 1973), 56-57.

man who had sighed after her, and carries him with her to enjoy Heaven for all eternity (*P. Silv. Razzi, part 3, mir. 60*). She makes a Cistercian monk, called Thomas, who ardently desired to see her, enjoy a paradise upon earth by her most sweet presence (*Diotall. tom. 2, Tratten. 16*). A poor monk is reduced almost to despair by scruples; she appears to him, and consoles him with these words: 'Why, my son, art thou overcome with grief, who hast so often wept with me in mine?' And to console him she takes him with her to Heaven (*P. Engelgrave, Dom. infra Oct. Nat. § 2*). Two religious of the order of St. Francis lose their way at night in the woods, and she provides them with a magnificent palace and delicious refreshments (*Nelle cron, apud Lig. Glor. of Mary*). She most gratefully restores to a priest his tongue, which the heretics had cut out because they found him saying Mass in her honor on Saturday (*Caesar. Dial. lib. 7, c. 24*). The brother of the King of Hungary is obliged by the people to be married; she makes her loving complaint to him while he is saying her office, at the Anthem, 'Thou art all fair': 'And if I am so fair and beautiful as thou sayest, why dost thou leave me for a far less beautiful spouse?' (*St. Anselm, in ep. apud Auriem, 1. 1, e. 8*).[225]

'The Holy Virgin acknowledges,' says Saint Bernard (*Serm. super Salve Regina*), 'and dearly loves them that love her, and she is near them that call upon her, especially those whom she sees like her in chastity and humility, and who, after her Divine Son, have placed their whole hope in her.' She desires to be loved; she goes before, entices, seeks after someone to give her his heart. She entreats him, 'My son, give me thy heart' (*Prov. 23:26*). 'She preventeth them that covet her, so that she first showeth herself unto them' (*Wisd. 6:14*). 'She seeks for those,' says the great Saint Bonaventure (*Stimul. Divin. Amor., p. 3, c. 16*), 'who devoutly and reverently approach her; these she cherishes, these she adopts as her children.' And, in fact, the demonstrations and expressions of love which Our Blessed Lady has deigned to use with her lovers, are most wonderful. They seem almost

---

[225] Roberto, *The Love of Mary*, 147-148.

incredible. In the preceding chapter we have related a great many, and we will give a few more here in confirmation of her loving gratitude and most partial tenderness towards whomsoever consecrates his heart to her love.[226]

Behold with what promptness and delight Mary returns the affection of them who love her! Unhappy that we are! We sometimes lose ourselves for creatures that value not, care not, for our affection, who are not pleased with our service, and perhaps contemn and laugh at our most passionate attachment to them, and our most heartfelt and tender expressions; and who are not even grateful for our valuable presents, which they consider simply their due. And shall we not resolve to love her who, possessing little less than infinite merit, yet loves us so tenderly, so earnestly desires our heart, is pleased with our affection, and responds to our love with the most obliging demonstrations of gratitude, the most constant fidelity, and who brings about effects which are the most advantageous to our highest interests? Let us no longer be so foolish. Let us love Mary, who alone can make us contented and happy in this world by her love, and forever blessed in the next by the enjoyment of her and of God."[227]

Gautier de Coinci

Relating the story of a knight to whom Mary appeared, Mary said to this knight:

"Friend, be not afraid...if I find you a loyal lover, there above, in Paradise, will you find me a loyal friend....Never for my sake strive in any tourney or deeds of chivalry, but if that you would be lord of my love, repeat an hundred and fifty Aves for a year without missing a day. Then you will win me without doubt, and thus will you hold and possess my whole love for ever and ever."[228]

---

[226] Roberto, *The Love of Mary*, 153-154.
[227] Roberto, *The Love of Mary*, 155.
[228] Fulton Brown, *Mary & the Art of Prayer*, 418.

"By God, let us not mismarry!...let us marry Mary, who marries her lovers to Heaven."[229]

Blessed James Alberione

"Mary's greatest glory, however, is in the changing of sinners to saints. She not only puts them back on the right path, but, if they do not resist, she strives to transform them into vessels of election and to make them saints.

She granted great favors to Margaret of Cortona, who was a sinner; to Mary of Egypt, famous for her dissolute life; to William of Aquitania, noted for his cruelty: Mary made them saints."[230]

Fr. Januarius Concilio

"Her love, always so tender, so energetic, so violent, intensified yet more by the spectacle of such tenderness and compassion [her crucified Son], becomes yet more tender, more powerful, more violent, and was raised, so to speak, to its highest power...Now, in this state in which Mary's heart, softened, melted by love, cannot but love—in this state in which her whole soul is a prey to the sweetest emotions, to the most tender affections, to the most powerful transports—in this very state our Blessed Lord, so to speak, catches her, and, in destining her to be our mother, bids her turn upon us that sentiment of immense tenderness, of most powerful love with which she was possessed at that moment. 'There stood by the cross of Jesus his

---

[229] Fulton Brown, *Mary & the Art of Prayer*, 419. This is meant in a supernatural/spiritual sense, it is not a reference to marriage of this world. For instance, St. Maximillian Kolbe considered consecration to Mary, in a general sense, as a "spousal union" (cf. Fr. Peter Fehlner's book *St. Maximilian M. Kolbe, Martyr of Charity: Pneumatologist, His Theology of the Holy Spirit*, page 147). Further, some men experience a mystical espousal to Mary, the complement to a woman's mystical espousal to Jesus; Saints such as Herman Joseph, John Eudes, and Blessed Alan de la Roche experienced this relatively rare grace.

[230] Alberione, *Glories and Virtues of Mary*, 206.

mother. And Jesus said: Woman, behold they Son.' It was as if he had said: 'O Woman! A most wondrous love causes thee to feel an unheard-of anguish. O woman! whom I observe a prey to the most tender and most impetuous feelings of love towards me, this very sentiment of a love so quick, so profound, so intense, so violent, which surrounds thee and fills thy whole being, I bid thee to turn towards my faithful. Behold in my disciple the whole Church; behold all faithful; to them thou must turn henceforth thy maternal love, because I put them in my place and will that thou shouldst consider them for what I am myself, thy only true Son. Behold thy son. From henceforth in them thou must find thy true Son, thy own Jesus…We and Jesus Christ are not loved as two different beings; we have become one with him—nay, we have taken his place, by his command, in the heart of Mary; and she who is the most glorious mother of God has become the most loving mother of men, loving us, by God's command, with the same love she felt for him."[231]

St. Jerome

"I affirm that even St. Joseph preserved his virginity through Mary…"[232]

Fr. Michael Gaitley

"We give, and she gives back infinitely more. We give her our sinful selves, and she gives us her Immaculate Heart. We give her our own meagre merits, and she not only augments and purifies them with her perfect love but gives us her infinitely greater merits and graces. We become empty after having given her all, and she fills us with the Spirit of God. She cares for our family, friends, and loved ones on our behalf—even better than we ourselves

---

[231] Januarius de Concilio, *The Knowledge of Mary* (New York: H.J. Hewitt, 1878), 238-240.
[232] Alberione, *Glories and Virtues of Mary*, 58.

can. She anticipates our needs and orders every detail of our lives for the greater glory of God. The path of holiness with her is "a path of roses and honey" compared to walking it without being consecrated to her. Indeed, she makes even our crosses and trials into something sweet. Moreover, she protects us from temptation and the attacks of the evil one."[233]

Richard of Saint Laurent

"Because wishing her servants to attain victory that they might win the crown, and knowing that only he who competes lawfully will be crowned (2 Timothy 2:5), she arranges wars and temptations for her lovers, and permits them to be afflicted from time to time. But with temptations she gives increase so that they are able to bear up, and she aids them with virtue that they might achieve the crown, for she is the one who gives strength to the weary with her prayers, merits, and examples."[234]

S.C. Biela

"Christ… 'entrusts' John to Mary, in the same way God entrusts a child to its mother. This act gives birth to her child. Mary lives in a singular union with him and loves him [and each person] as if he were her only child."[235]

"In the realization of her vocation as Mother of Jesus, Mary employed all her physical and spiritual forces. Totally and until the end, she binds herself in the prolongation of this vocation, which is her spiritual maternity with respect to us. She lives for us, takes care of us and is completely at our disposal. From the moment of our conception, Mary is present with each one of us—serves us through our earthly mothers for whom she intercedes

---

[233] Gaitley, *33 Days to Morning Glory*, 109-110.
[234] Fulton Brown, *Mary & the Art of Prayer*, 393.
[235] S.C. Biela, *In the Arms of Mary* (Orange, CA: IN the Arms of Mary Foundation, 2005), 159.

to obtain the necessary graces. She is closer to us more than our earthly mothers, whose possibilities are limited. The heavenly Mother is continually 'at the disposal' of each of her children; she is disposed to help every time they call upon her.

When you begin to look at your life in the light of faith, you will discover that it was she who watched over you in the night, who fed you and took care of you, who watched over you in every moment of your life. She cared for you through the doctor who treated you. It was she who showed you love through all the persons who did something good for you.

It was through her intercession that you encountered so much kindness and affection.

Mary is continually with you and takes care of your integral development. In a special way, she takes care of your spiritual growth."[236]

"Mary, who was given to us as our Mother, carried Christ in her arms. We have the right to think that she 'carries us in her arms', also... 'Behold, your mother' (Jn 19:27) can be interpreted as: John, from today you have the special right to benefit from the privilege of being Mary's child—this privilege consists of being 'carried in the arms of My mother' who is also your Mother. When you contemplate an image of Mary, you can always remember that you are in her arms like Jesus was—and this is not an exaggeration."[237]

"Whether that with which you occupy yourself is important or insignificant, you are always in her arms. 'In her arms' you work, you eat, you drink coffee. 'In her arms' you fall asleep and you sleep.'"[238]

---

[236] Biela, *In the Arms of Mary*, 169.
[237] Biela, *In the Arms of Mary*, 170-171.
[238] Biela, *In the Arms of Mary*, 174.

Fr. Stefano Manelli

"Furthermore, if we reflect that Jesus, the fruit of Mary's immaculate womb, is the whole of Mary's love, of Her sweetness, all of Her intimacy, of Her riches, of Her whole life, then when we receive Him we cannot not receive Her as well, who, by bonds of highest love, and by bonds of flesh and blood, forms with Jesus a single alliance of love, one whole, as She is always and inseparably 'leaning upon her Beloved' (Cant. 8:5)."[239]

"And so 'the Eucharist,' writes St. Albert the Great, 'produces impulses of angelic love and has the singular capacity of effecting in souls a holy, instinctive tenderness for the Queen of Angels. She has given us Flesh of her Flesh and Bone of her Bone, and in the Eucharist She continues to give us this sweet, virginal, Heavenly food.'"[240]

"Mary can quite rightfully beckon us and speak to us in the inspired words of Solomon, "Come and eat my bread, drink the wine I have prepared for you' (Prov 9:5)."[241]

"What shall we say of Our Lady's charity on Calvary, where she was willing to see her Son slain for the sake of us sinners? *'Greater love than this no man hath, that a man lay down his life for his friends'* (J. 15:13). Our Lady would have greatly preferred, many times over, to take her Son's place. She, in fact, consented to feel the most terrible sufferings of Jesus' physical crucifixion, all for our sake. She could not have been more generous with us."[242]

---

[239] Stefano Manelli, *Jesus Our Eucharistic Love* (New Bedford, MA: Academy of the Immaculate, 1996), 107.

[240] Manelli, *Jesus Our Eucharistic Love*, 108.

[241] Manelli, *Jesus Our Eucharistic Love*, 113.

[242] Manelli, *Devotion to Our Lady*, 135.

St. Veronica Giuliani

"She was Coadjutrix in our Redemption and suffered within herself, by way of participation, each pain, sorrow, anguish and agony which Jesus would have to undergo, not only in these 24 hours of His most holy Passion, but in the entire course of His life. For both of them it was 33 years of the most painful torment and the Most Holy Virgin was always participating in all His suffering..."[243]

"...she, in her virginal body, had participated in all the sufferings of the Passion and Death of the Son and was made Coadjutrix of our Redemption..."[244]

"...all that the Son was doing, she was doing; all that the Son was suffering, she was suffering; but the greatest pains were those deep within the soul and the heart."[245]

[243] Mother Maria Francesca Perillo, "Marian Coredemption in St. Veronica Giuliani," in *Mary at the Foot of the Cross, Acts of the International Symposium on Marian Coredemption* (New Bedford, MA: Academy of the Immaculate, 2001), 246.
[244] Perillo, "Marian Coredemption in St. Veronica Giuliani," 249.
[245] Perillo, "Marian Coredemption in St. Veronica Giuliani," 253-254.

IV

Mary Longs for Your Love: An Anonymous 15th Century Poem

The Virgin's Complaint

Quia Amore Langueo
[Because I languish for Love]
(Or, *The Virgin's Complaint*)

Within a chamber of a tower,
As musing on the moon stood I,
A Queen with honour crowned and power
Me thought I saw, enthroned on high.
She made her plaint with bitter cry,
For soul of man by sin brought low:
I may not leave mankind to die,
Quia amore langueo

I look for love of man my brother,
And plead for him in every guise,
His Mother I, who can no other,
Why should I my dear child despise?
Though he offend me divers wise
Through fleshly frailty falling so,
Yet must I rue until he rise,
Quia amore langueo.

I wait and bide with longing great;
I love and look till man shall crave;
I plain for pity of his state;
Would he ask for grace 'twere his to have:
Call on me, Soul, thee will I save,
Child, bid me come, and I will go;
Thou ne're didst pray, but I forgave,
Quia amore langueo.

Mother of Mercy I was made,
For thee who need'st it to illume:
More fain am I to grant its aid
Than thee to ask; why mute in gloom?
When said I nay? tell me to whom?
Ne're yet, indeed, to friend or foe;
When ye ask not, I weep your doom,
Quia amore langueo.

O wretch on earth, I look on thee
And see the trespass day by day,
With sin against my purity,
With pride against my meek array:
My love thee waits, wrath is away;
My love thee calls; from me wilt thou go?
I prithee, sinner, to me pray.
Quia amore langueo.

My Son was outlawed for thy sin,
And scourged for trespass of thine;
It pricks my heart so near my Kin

Should be so used. Ah, son of mine,
Thy Father is the Son benign
My breast hath fed; He loved thee so,
He died for thee; my heart is thine,
Quia amore langueo.

My Son hath suffered for thy love;

His heart was pierced with a spear;
To bring thy soul to heaven above
For love of thee so died He here.
Therefore thou art to me most dear,
Since my Son hath loved thee so;
Thou ne'er dost pray but I thee hear.
Quia amore langueo.

My Son hath granted for thy sake
Each grace that I to ask am fain,
For He no vengeance wills to take,
If I for thee crave amain:
Then mercy ask, thou shalt obtain,
I with such ruth look on thy woe;
I long for mercy thou shouldst plain,
Quia amore langueo.[246]

---

[246] M. Therese, *I Sing of a Maiden*, 112-114.

Appendix

Cor ad Cor Loquitur: Blank pages to add one's own "letters" to Mary

Cor ad Cor Loquitur

Cor ad Cor Loquitur

Cor ad Cor Loquitur

Cor ad Cor Loquitur

Cor ad Cor Loquitur

Cor ad Cor Loquitur

Bibliography

Alberione, James. *Glories and Virtues of Mary*. Trans. Hilda Calabro. Boston: Daughters of St. Paul, 1982.

Alighieri, Dante. Trans. Mark Musa. *Paradise*. New York: Penguin, 1984.

Barthas, Chanoine and G. Da Fonseca, *Our Lady of Light*. Milwaukee: Bruce, 1948.

Baij, Maria Cecilia. *The Life of Saint Joseph*. Asbury, NJ: 101 Foundation, 2000.

Ball, Ann. *Modern Saints, Their Lives and Faces: Book Two*. Rockford, IL: TAN, 1990.

Bernard of Clairvaux, *St. Bernard's Sermons on the Blessed Virgin Mary*. Chulmleigh, Devon: Augustine, 1987.

Berubé, Keith. *Mary, the Beloved*. St. Louis, MO: En Route, 2017.

Berubé, Keith. *Mary: The Rosary, the Relationship, and Dragons*. St. Louis, MO: En Route, 2020.

Biela, S.C. *In the Arms of Mary*. Orange, CA: In the Arms of Mary Foundation, 2005.

Bloomfield, William. "The Daily Sayings of St. Philip Neri," at Sacred Art Series Blog, at http://sacredartseries.blogspot.com.

Bonaventure. *The Mirror of the Blessed Virgin Mary*. EWTN: at www.ewtn.com.

Boston Catholic Journal, "The Little Office of the Blessed Virgin Mary." Boston Catholic Journal: at www.boston-catholic-journal.com.

Brown, Raphael. *Saints Who Saw Mary*. Charlotte, NC: TAN, 2012.

Brown, Raphael. *The Life of Mary as Seen by the Mystics*. Charlotte, NC: TAN, 2012.

Calloway, Donald. *Champions of the Rosary: The History and Heroes of a Spiritual Weapon.* Stockbridge, MA: Marian, 2016.

Concilio, Januarius. *The Knowledge of Mary.* New York: H.J. Hewitt, 1878.

Gabriele Cingolani, *Saint Gabriel Possenti, Passionist: A Young Man in Love.* New York: Alaba, 2001.

Dallaire, Glenn. "St Gemma and Her Guardian Angel." St Gemma Galgani: at http://www.stgemmagalgani.com.

Dallaire, Glenn. "The Blessed Virgin Mary and St Gemma Galgani." St Gemma Galgani: at www.stgemmagalgani.com.

De Montfort, Louis. *True Devotion.* Trans. Frederick William Faber. Rockford, IL: TAN, 1985.

Eudes, John. *The Admirable Heart of Mary.* New York: P.J. Kenedy & Sons, 1948.

Flores, Deyanira. "The Rich Mariological Doctrine of the Nican Mopohua." Marian Congress: at www.mariancongress.org.

Francis of Assisi. "A Salutation to the Blessed Virgin Mary." Franciscan Archive: at http://franciscan-archive.org/franciscana/prayers.html.

Fulton Brown, Rachel. *Mary & the Art of Prayer: The Hours of the Virgin in Medieval Christian Life and Thought.* New York: Columbia, 2018.

Gaitley, Michael. *33 Days to Morning Glory.* Stockbridge, MA: Marian, 2013.

Gaynor, John. *The Life of St. Vincent Pallotti.* Boston, MA: St. Paul Editions, 1980.

Hollobough, Camillus. *St. Gabriel, Passionist.* New York: Catholic Book Publishing, 1953.

Hopkins, Gerard Manley. "The Blessed Virgin Compared to the Air We Breathe." Bartleby: at www.bartleby.com.

Iannelli, Maria Gabriella. "The Mediation of the Blessed Virgin Mary in the lives of Blessed Francisco and Jacinta of Fatima." In *Mary at the Foot of the Cross, VII: Acts of the Seventh International Symposium on Marian*

Coredemption, 440-471. New Bedford, MA: Academy of the Immaculate, 2008.

Jamart, Francoise. *Complete Spiritual Doctrine of St. Therese of Lisieux.* Staten Island, NY: Alba House, 1961.

Johnston, Francis. *The Wonder of Guadalupe: The Origin and Cult of the Miraculous Image of the Blessed Virgin in Mexico.* Rockford, IL: TAN, 1981.

Joseph, John. "Lady of the Snow." Ten-Stringed Lyre of the New Israel (10 October 2015): at http://tenstringedlyreofthenewisrael.blogspot.in/.

Joseph, John. "Snow White: An Allegory of the Blessed Virgin Mary." Ten-Stringed Lyre of the New Israel (22 August 2016): at http://tenstringedlyreofthenewisrael.blogspot.in/.

Laurentin, Rene. *Dictionnaire des Apparitions.* Paris: Fayard, 2006.

Kaczmarek, Louis. *Mary and the Power of God's Love* . Manassas, VA: Trinity, 1988.

Kanjiramkalayil, Mathew. "The Role of Mary in the Holiness of St. Vincent Pallotti." Pallotti Institute: at www.pallottiinstitute.com.

Kempis, Thomas. *The Imitation of Mary.* Westminster, MD: Newman, 1961.

Kirby, Mark. "Maria Bambina." Vultus Christi (2008): at vultus.stblogs.org.

Kolbe, Maximillian. "A Rule of Life for Those Consecrated to the Immaculate Virgin." Franciscan Archive: at http://franciscan-archive.org/franciscana/prayers.html.

Knox, Ronald. "The Priestly Life." EWTN (1958): at http://ewtn.com.

Lasserre, M. Henri. *Bernadette.* Derby, England: Richardson and Son: 1879.

Liguori, Alphonsus. *The Glories of Mary.* Rockford, IL: TAN, 1977.

Lord, Bob and Penny. *The Many Faces of Mary: A Love Story.* Journeys of Faith, 1987.

Manelli, Stefano. *Devotion to Our Lady.* New Bedford, MA: Academy of the Immaculate, 2001.

Manelli, Stefano. *Jesus Our Eucharist Love.* New Bedford, MA: The Academy of the Immaculate, 2008.

Manelli, Stefano. *The Marian Vow.* New Bedford, MA: Academy of the Immaculate, 2010.

Margerie, Bertrand. "The Knowledge of Mary and the Sacrifice of Jesus." In *Mary at the Foot of the Cross,* 31-40. New Bedford, MA: Academy of the Immaculate, 2001.

Martin, Therese. *The Poetry of Saint Thérèse of Lisieux.* Trans. Donald Kinney. Washington, DC: ICS, 1996.

Mary of Agreda. *Divine Mysteries of the Most Holy Rosary.* Necedah, WI: J.M.J. Book, 1979.

Montes De Oca, V. *More About Fatima.* Manchester, UK: C. Nicholls, Philips Park, 1971.

"Mother of Mercy (Pellevoisin, France)." *365 Days with Mary.* at www.mariancalendar.org.

Pastrovicchi, Angelo. *St. Joseph of Copertino.* Rockford, IL: TAN, 1980.

Pelletier, Joseph. *The Sun Danced at Fatima.* Garden City, NY: Image, 1983.

Perillo, Mo Maria Francesca. "Marian Coredemption in St. Veronica Giuliani." In *Mary at the Foot of the Cross, Acts of the International Symposium on Marian Coredemption,* 237-265. New Bedford, MA: Academy of the Immaculate, 2001.

Perrin, Xavier. *The Radiance of Her Face.* Trans. Laetitia Payne. Kettering OH: Angelico, 2017.

Peyton, Patrick. *All for Her.* Hollywood, CA: Family Theater, 1973.

Pierre, Mary. *Mary was Her Life.* New York: Benziger, 1960.

Poe, Edgar Allan. "Hymn." The Complete Poems of Edger Allan Poe, The University of Adelaide: at https://ebooks.adelaide.edu.au.

Sa-onoy, Modesto P. "Holy Rosary—A Super Weapon." The Daily Guardian: at https://thedailyguardian.net.

Schoeman, Roy. "Jewish Harvard Professor Roy Schoeman Becomes Convinced Catholic (Talk 1 Prescott Mission)." Salvation is from the Jews (24 February 2014): at www.youtube.com.

Schoeman, Roy. "Virgin Mary appears to Harvard Professor Part 1 (Jewish Convert to Catholic)." YouTube (11 April 2015): at www.youtube.com.

Servants of the Pierced Hearts of Jesus and Mary. "Apparition of the Virgin Mary in Beauraing, Belgium." Servants of the Pierced Hearts of Jesus and Mary: at www.piercedhearts.org.

Shakespeare, William. "The Merchant of Venice." In *The Complete Works of William Shakespeare*, 245-274.Glasgow: HarperCollins, 2006.

Sheen, Fulton. "Mary, Motherhood and the Home." Catholic Truth Society Pamphlets: at http://pamphlets.org.au.

Sheen, Fulton. *The World's First Love*. San Francisco: Ignatius, 2010.

Therese, M. *I Sing of a Maiden: The Mary Book of Verse*. New York: Macmillan, 1947.

The Douay-Rheims Bible. Rockford: TAN, 1989.

"The Message." *Ngome Marian Shrine*: at https://ngome.wordpress.com/

"The Messages of Cuapa." *The Miracle Hunter*: at http://www.miraclehunter.com/.

"The Messages of Pellevoisin." *The Miracle Hunter*: at http://www.miraclehunter.com.

Thompson, Francis. "The After Woman." In *The Works of Francis Thompson, Poems: Volume II*. NY: Charles Scribner's Sons, 1913.

Trochu, Francois. *Saint Bernadette Soubirous*. Charlotte, NC: TAN, 2012.

Vost, Kevin. *St. Albert the Great: Champion of Faith & Reason*. Charlotte, NC: TAN, 2011.

Walsh, C. Lourdes. *The Story of Our Lady of Guadalupe*. Tampa, FL: Mirandapro, 2005.

Werferl, Franz. *The Song of Bernadette*. San Francisco: Ignatius, 2006.

Williamson, Benedict. *Gemma of Lucca*. St. Louis: Alexander-Ouseley Ltd and B. Herder, 1932.

Made in the USA
Monee, IL
16 August 2021